Causal Asymmetry
& the
Explanatory Constraint

Zhiheng Tang

Cranmore Publications

Copyright © 2011 by Zhiheng Tang

All rights reserved. This book, or parts thereof, may not be reproduced in any form without permission.

A catalogue record for this book is available from the British Library

ISBN: 978-1-907962-41-7

Published by Cranmore Publications

Reading, England

www.cranmorepublications.co.uk

This book is dedicated to my grandmother

Mrs. Liang

I wish to acknowledge my great indebtedness to, first of all, Professor David Oderberg, without whose generous and constant encouragement and support this book would never have been possible; to Professor David Owens, who provided me with valuable advice with regard to the last two chapters; to Chris "the philoseraptor" Pulman, who did the proof-reading and made careful and highly pertinent comments; to all the participants at my presentations in the Graduate Seminar in the Department of Philosophy at the University of Reading; and to my wife, Jintao Feng, who takes care of everything else.

Contents

Introduction 9

1 Causal Asymmetry and Conditionality 17

2 Causal Asymmetry and Causal Forks 42

3 Borderline Cases (I): Simultaneous Causation and Backwards Causation 111

4 Borderline Cases (II): Absence Causation 147

5 The Explanatory Constraint on Causation 195

Bibliography 239

Introduction

The connection between the two topics in the book's title, 'Causal Asymmetry and the Explanatory Constraint', is one that immediately becomes clear once both topics are properly understood. Let me then explain the two topics in turn.

The relation between cause and effect is generally thought to be asymmetric, in that if C causes E, then E does not cause C. (C and E are names of causal relata, be they objects, events, facts, tropes, etc. Throughout the book I do not take sides on the nature of causal relata. For brevity, most of the time I speak of events as causal relata, unless the nature of causal relata itself is under discussion.) Put alternatively, the idea is that for any causal relation between two entities, the cause is prior to the effect in a way that the effect is not prior to the cause. Moreover, in view of the fact that to distinguish between cause and effect is just to identify such a priority, the idea is simply that for any causal relation there is a cause-effect distinction to this relation. These formulations are slightly different in meaning, but throughout the book I shall use the term 'causal asymmetry' interchangeably with 'causal priority', as well as with 'the cause-effect distinction', such that they are all meant to name the kind of thing commonly marked out in these formulations.

This 'kind of thing' is something we know to be there, but often we have no clear and firm grasp of it. Causal asymmetry is thus in need of analysis. An easy approach to analyzing it is to say that the asymmetry at issue is simply a temporal one. Hume famously incorporates temporal priority into his definition of cause. And if so it may be thought that nothing other than temporal asymmetry between cause and effect is needed to account for causal asymmetry. But to analyze causal asymmetry in terms of the temporal asymmetry between cause and effect is inadequate in at least the following two respects. First, it will make both the notion of simultaneous causation and that of backwards causation analytically nonsense. But they are not. People often argue in sensible ways that there are cases of simultaneous causation. Even backwards causation makes initial sense, or at any rate it is not something that should be ruled out a priori. Second, according to the so-called causal theory of time, which some think to be plausible, the asymmetry of time is analyzable in terms of the asymmetry of causation rather

Introduction

than the converse. However problematic this theory may be, it does not seem to be a non-starter.

The first aim of this book, then, is to give an account of causal asymmetry without appealing to the temporal asymmetry that may exist between cause and effect. (On some occasions, when I do need to mention this temporal asymmetry, I reserve the term 'causal direction' for it.) Note, however, that it is not my aim to give a general theory of causation, even though in my view an appropriate account of causal asymmetry will facilitate such a theory. Looking from the other end, some may say that a good general theory of causation should have enough resources to account for casual asymmetry. This is an issue I shall focus on in Chs. 1 and 2. In these two chapters, I shall have a critical look at whether, within the framework of two major theories of causation, causal asymmetry can be adequately analyzed. The answer turns out to be negative. So in Ch. 3, by studying two 'borderline' cases of causation—i.e., simultaneous causation and backwards causation—I shall present my own view of causal asymmetry, arguing that casual asymmetry consists in explanatory asymmetry. More precisely, the idea is that C causes E, only if C explains E but not the other way around.

Ch. 4 takes us to the second topic of this book. To see how, a piece of autobiographical information should be in place. I began writing the book having in mind that causal asymmetry is a relatively isolated topic in philosophy of causation, and thus can be adequately discussed without getting into areas I was not fully confident of managing. In a sense I believe I was right. I still think that a simple truth about casual asymmetry is that it is the explanatory asymmetry between cause and effect. But on the way to reaching this conclusion I chose to examine some borderline cases, one of which is absence causation—i.e., an alleged casual relation in which absences, or omissions, are regarded as relata. In discussing absence causation, however, I found myself inevitably pushed to address some basic issues about causation in general, not just about causal asymmetry.

For example, in a crude sense absences are nothing. And from this it follows that in a putative case of absence causation a connection between absences is itself also nothing—at least, nothing physical. This is astonishing. Of course, it may be argued for various reasons (some of which will be discussed in Ch. 4) that absence causation is just an illusion. But this is not the point surprising us. The point is how come such a kind of relation between

Introduction

absences—a relation such that there are neither relata nor a physical connection between any relata—can be in any sensible way regarded as causal in the first place. Absence causation does make initial, prima facie, sense; otherwise we would too often feel uneasy when people talked about things like being dehydrated to death, fire due to negligence, prevention of a crisis, and so on. But why?

It is my conviction that if absence causation can even just make prima facie sense, there must be something fundamental to our concept of causation such that a notion as unusual as that of absence causation, as long as it satisfies this something, will start to gain plausibility. I suggest that this something, put positively, is a relation's being explanatory is conceptually prior its being causal; negatively, it is what I shall call the explanatory *Constraint* on causation.

Now, the conclusion of the first part of the book—that causal asymmetry is to be identified with the explanatory asymmetry between cause and effect—can be seen as an inference from *Constraint*. But the order of this inference is not the order of my argument. I hope that even if *Constraint* is contentious, my discussion of causal asymmetry can be judged independently of this thesis. At any rate, it appears that one can hold the view that causal asymmetry consists in explanatory asymmetry without also holding the stronger view that explanation is conceptually prior to causation.

There are some obvious objections to *Constraint*. Causation is generally thought to be extensional, transitive and, less generally but still popularly, intrinsic (to causal relata and their properties). On the face of it, all of these views are more or less incompatible with *Constraint*. To address these views is a huge task I cannot undertake in this book, so it has to wait for another occasion. Instead, in Ch. 5, I shall address an objection made by causal theorists of explanation against *Constraint*, and try to make a case for *Constraint* by considering the problem of selection (with relation to 'the cause' as opposed to 'a cause'). With these efforts, together with my argument for causal asymmetry as explanatory asymmetry, I hope to offer limited support for *Constraint*.

So much for the title and the plan of the book. Before moving on to Ch. 1, I want to say a few words about some notable theories of causation I do not touch upon in this book. First, there is a kind of theory that we may call the energy-flow theory (e.g. Fair [1979] and

Dowe [2000]). Roughly, the idea of this theory is to define causation in terms of some kind of transfer of energy, or other preferred physical quantities. It is not that I think that an energy-flow theorist will have nothing to say about causal asymmetry. Actually, it appears that the theorist will have something very straightforward to say, presumably something like 'C causes E but E does not C, just in case there is a transfer of energy from C to E but not E to C'. I choose to bypass this theory's account of causal asymmetry, because generally speaking I think it is a defective theory of causation, suffering not only from circularity but also some intractable counterexamples (e.g., turning off a light). For similar reasons, I will not be concerned with the manipulation theory of causation. Under this theory, suppose we say that C causes E but not vice versa, in the sense that C could be brought about by doing E but E could not be brought about by doing C (von Wright [1971]). It seems to me that this account, despite its neat appearance, is grounded on a theory of causation whose central notions—i.e. bringing-about and doing—cannot be understood unless causation is already intelligible.

For different reasons, another notable theory of causation I choose to ignore is the probabilistic theory.

Technical details and various ways to construe the notion of probability aside, the basic idea of this theory is simple and clear: C causes E, if and only if in a certain sense C makes E more probable. While I have not much to say for or against the theory as a theory about *general* causation, I seriously doubt that the theory without some significant inputs from other major theories of causation (in particular, the counterfactual theory) can adequately analyze *singular* causal relations. It appears to me that the notion of probability is intrinsically associated with *types* (of events, facts, etc.), and if possible at all can only in a derivative sense apply to singular cases of causation. Causal asymmetry, however, is a feature of singular causation not in any obvious way inherited from the asymmetry of general causation. Even in an utterly simple world—say, a world in which only two particles exist and one collides into another—still the causal asymmetry of the collision holds. Based on these considerations, I decide to set aside the probabilistic theory of causation as well.

Chapter 1

Causal Asymmetry and Conditionality

1.1 Causal Asymmetry and the Regularity Theory

1.2 Causal Asymmetry and Conditionality

1.1 Causal Asymmetry and the Regularity Theory

Hume famously defined a cause as 'an object precedent and contiguous to another, and where all the objects resembling the former are placed in a like relation of priority and contiguity to those objects that resemble the latter' [*Treatise*, Book I, Part III, Sect. XIV].[1] While a lot

---

[1] As we all know Hume defined causation in several different ways, and some have quite different connotations. Notably, he also gave a counterfactual definition, which we will touch upon in the next chapter.

of things can be said, and have been said, about this definition, few of them are relevant to a discussion of causal asymmetry.[2] As explained in the Introduction, the temporal asymmetry (in Hume's definition, 'priority') between a cause and its effect is neither equivalent to the causal asymmetry between them nor is it responsible for this asymmetry. Also, the question whether a cause has to be contiguous to its effect, which I doubt, is not our concern, because the relation of contiguity is apparently symmetric—if A is contiguous to B, then B is contiguous to A. Arguably, by stressing the *resemblance* among causes and that among effects Hume's definition implies some kind of causal relation between types. But, again, the consideration of causation between types is not relevant to this investigation—causal asymmetry can exist between tokens, as much as it can exist between types. And, finally, the central notion of Hume's theory of causation, the notion of regularity or constant conjunction (as indicated by Hume's use of the phrase, 'a *like* relation') does not seem to imply any asymmetric relation between cause and effect: the regularity or constant

---

[2] For a detailed exegesis of Hume's account of causation, see Mackie [1974: Ch. 1].

conjunction between A-type and B-type events is one and the same constant conjunction between B-type and A-type events. There is nothing asymmetric whatsoever in conjunctions of this kind.

But Hume's definition provides a platform on which a bundle of similar theories of causation can be developed; and some of these theories may shed light on the notion of causal asymmetry. By providing a formal analysis of causal regularity—i.e., by analyzing causal regularity in terms of conditionality—Mill makes a considerable improvement upon Hume's theory. 'The cause', says Mill [*System of Logic*, Book III, Ch. 5, Sect. 3], 'is the sum total of the conditions positive and negative taken together...which being realized, the consequent invariably follows.' It is easy to see that Mill takes a cause to be a *sufficient* condition of its effect. Note, however, that the cause contains also all the *necessary* conditions that are 'equally indispensable for the production of the consequent' [ibid.]. Thus, according to Mill, the regularity instantiated by a cause-effect connection consists in the fact that the cause is a condition that is both necessary and sufficient ('NS' for short) for the effect. No doubt, a lot of questions can be raised about this analysis.[3] It is, however, not my purpose to evaluate Mill's analysis or any other varieties of the regularity theory, *for their own sake*. Suffice to say that Mill's analysis cannot be helpful in accounting for causal asymmetry. If A is a NS condition of B, it follows immediately that B is also a NS condition of A.[4] There is

---

[3] For one thing, by interpreting the Cause as both necessary and sufficient for its effect Mill's analysis appears to be too strong, since normally we don't take all the causally necessary factors prior to a certain object, especially negative ones, to be part of its cause. In what sense can it be said that my refraining from smashing the computer in front of me is part of the cause of my finishing this chapter?

[4] As noted before I use capital letters as dummy names generally for events, properties, facts, states of affairs, etc. In talking about conditions this kind of use may cause some uneasiness. While conditions can be properties, whether they can be facts or states of affairs is problematic, and even more so whether they can be events. It seems that we talk about events or states of affairs as conditions only insofar as there are correspondingly *kinds* of events or states of affairs as conditions. The problem, though interesting on its own [Kim 1971], will not in any significant way affect my argument here and after. For peace of mind we can, when appropriate, read A, for example, as something of which event/state A is a kind.

no place to accommodate causal asymmetry in Mill's analysis either.

A much subtler analysis of causation in terms of necessary and/or sufficient conditions is Mackie's INUS condition analysis. In observing that in most cases a single cause-factor, *by itself*, is neither necessary nor sufficient for the effect to follow, J. L. Mackie [1965: 34] suggests that we should understand a cause as 'an *insufficient* but *necessary* part of a condition which is itself *unnecessary* but *sufficient* for the result' (INUS condition for short). For example, we can say that the burning of a cigarette caused a fire. Even though the burning is by itself insufficient for the fire (other things, like dryness of the air, inflammable materials nearby, non-presence of a fireman, and so on, are required), it is a necessary part of the sum of all the actual conditions that led to the fire. On the other hand, the sum of all the actual conditions on that occasion, though sufficient for the fire, is unnecessary for it (in other words, some other possible combinations of conditions could also have led to the fire). But whether or not Mackie's analysis of causal regularity is plausible or not is beside the point, for I am not here to evaluate the analysis itself. Mackie's analysis is of little use in accounting for causal asymmetry. As we said about Mill's NS conditional analysis, given that A is a NS condition of B it follows that B is also a NS condition of A. It can similarly be proved that, if A is an INUS condition of B, B is also an INUS condition of A. Suppose that A is an INUS condition of B, and let X be a combination of some other conditions, positive and negative, which, together with A, is sufficient for B. The causal relation can then be written as, in symbols, (A&X)→B. Furthermore, suppose that when *A* does not obtain, some alternative combinations of conditions can also lead to *B*. For the purpose of this argument we don't really need to unpack these alternative combinations, so we can just treat them as a single factor and represent it as Y. Now, it is easy to see that A&XvY constitutes the necessary and sufficient condition for *B*—in symbols, ((A&X)vY)↔B. From this it follows that (B&¬Y)→A, which obviously means that B together with the non-obtaining of Y is sufficient for A. Suppose that some other combinations of conditions, the whole set of which we represent as Z, are also sufficient for A. Then we get ((B&¬Y)vZ)↔A. Obviously, according to the definition of an INUS condition, B is here an INUS condition of A. So it is proved that from the fact that A is an INUS condition of B it follows that B is also an INUS condition of A.[5]

Mackie [1974: 161] is well aware that the relation between an INUS condition and its effect is not asymmetric, and that for this reason it cannot be used to account for causal asymmetry. Indeed, he emphasizes in several places that what is ideal is an appropriate conditional analysis of causation *plus* an appropriate account of causal asymmetry. Besides the INUS-analysis, he separately comes up with an account of causal asymmetry ('causal priority', as he calls it), which he [1974: 190] puts as follows:

> Suppose that X and Y are individual events, and X is seen as necessary (and sufficient) in the circumstances for Y, so that the basic requirement for the judgment that X caused Y is met. Then, despite this, X was not causally prior to Y if there was a time at which Y was fixed while X was unfixed. If, on the other hand, X was fixed at a time when Y was un-

---

[5] Essentially the same proof has been suggested by Mackie [1974: 161] and Papineau [1985: 279].

fixed, then X was causally prior to Y. Again, if X was not fixed until it occurred, then even if Y also was fixed as soon as X occurred (given, of course, that X was necessary in the circumstances for Y), X was causally prior to Y. And further, if there is some line or chain of causation, some continuous causal process, linking X and Y and some other event Z so that X was between Y and Z, and if Z was not fixed until it occurred, then X was causally prior to Y.

Unfortunately this account isn't successful. Many powerful objections have been raised against it, claiming that it relies too much on the notion of temporal priority, is ambiguous, or even it is incoherent.[6] I will examine two of these objections here, both pointed out by Michael Tooley [1987].

The first problem with Mackie's account is that, if causal determinism is true (this is to say, roughly, that given the laws of nature any event is necessitated by any

---

[6] See, for example, Sanford [1976: 194-5], Brown [1979: 336-8] and Tooley [1987: 217-8].

another), then according to Mackie's account all events are fixed. Since there is no room left for unfixed events, the notion of causal priority, as Mackie understands it, would become vacuous. Mackie [1974: 191] noticed this problem, but was happy to say that '[i]f you have too much causation, it destroys one of its most characteristic features [that is, causal priority]'. But unless one has already endorsed Mackie's account, there don't seem to be any compelling reason to think that causal determinism and causal asymmetry are opposed to one another. Furthermore, as Tooley [1987: 217] pointed out, 'it [would be] rather surprising if our ordinary concept of causation has the consequence that it is logically necessary that some events be causally undetermined'.

The second problem for Mackie's account can be illustrated by referring to an example suggested by Douglas Gasking [1955: 479]. Suppose that a piece of iron begins to glow when its temperature reaches 1,000 °C, and never glows except at or above this temperature—in other words, the iron's reaching 1,000 °C is both necessary and sufficient for its glowing. The relation exemplified the glowing and the temperature of the iron is thus similar to that between X and Y in Mackie's account. Since it appears that there is no spatiotemporal gap between the iron's glowing and its reaching 1,000 °C (there is no time and no place at which one of them occurs whereas the other does not), and since the glowing and its reaching 1,000 °C are both necessary and sufficient for each other (from either of them the other can be *inferentially* fixed), it seems to follow that, according to Mackie's account, there is no causal asymmetry whatsoever between the iron's glowing and its reaching 1,000 °C. But this result is quite counterintuitive. It is natural (and surely also correct) to think that it is the iron's reaching 1,000 °C that causes it to glow, but not the other way around.[7] So, Mackie's account of causal asymmetry is, at best, incomplete, for it cannot account for the causal asymmetry in relations like that between the iron's glowing and its reaching 1,000 °C.

---

[7] This argument, Tooley admitted, is *not* very useful for him. Obviously, in the example the kind of causation between the iron's reaching 1,000 °C and its glowing is supposed to be simultaneous one. Since Tooley does not think there are real cases of simultaneous causation, he cannot make much out of this example without endangering his own position on simultaneous causation. I, by contrast, am fairly open to the possibility of simultaneous causation.

2.2 Causal Asymmetry and Conditionality

So far, neither Hume's original analysis of causation in terms of regularity nor its variants in the form of Mill's NS condition analysis or Mackie's INUS condition analysis has been found to contain any elements that can be used to account for the asymmetry of causation. But there are still some moves that a proponent of the Humean theory of causation might make to address this shortfall. In claiming that Mackie's INUS analysis fails to provide an account of causal asymmetry I treated the causal connective as a truth-functional conditional. However, this treatment is notoriously controversial, and most likely wrong.[8] Less controversially, but still questionably, in discussing Mill's analysis I took it for granted that A's being a NS condition of B entails B's also being a NS condition of A, and thus concluded that there is no built-in asymmetry in NS conditionality. Although this assumption is commonly made in most logic textbooks, the bi-conditional poorly represents our ordinary understanding of NS conditionality. Suppose, for example, that until Tom's death his wife Janie has him as

---

[8] See Davidson [1967: Sect. 1].

her only husband. Tom's death is thought to be a NS condition of Janie's becoming a widow, but from this it does not follow, as it would be strange to say, that Janie's becoming a widow is a NS condition of Tom's death. It appears that our ordinary conception of the NS conditionality between Tom's death and Janie's becoming a widow means something quite different from the mutual implication between the fact that Tom dies and the fact that Janie becomes a widow, a mutual implication which, though generally taken to be legitimate, is only sanctioned by logicians' restrictive use of 'necessary and sufficient condition'.

That there is a considerable discrepancy between the logician's treatment of necessary and/or sufficient conditions and our natural understanding of them was noticed by Wertheimer [1968]. Wertheimer tried to clarify the notions of necessary condition and sufficient conditions, and argued that necessary and/or sufficient conditionals should not be understood merely truth-functionally. In the remaining part of this chapter I will look into some details of Wertheimer's discussion, locate an element of truth in his discussion with respect to the problem of causal asymmetry, and explain why his discussion is far from adequate in solving the problem facing Humean theories of causation.

Wertheimer begins his discussion by challenging a widely held view that the assumed equivalence between A's being a sufficient condition of B and B's being a necessary condition of A should be interpreted as the equivalence, in propositional logic, between $a \rightarrow b$ and $\neg b \rightarrow \neg a$ (according to Wertheimer, a and b are sentences which are used to assert the existence of states of affairs, of which A and B are names). The logical equivalence between the two material implications is acceptable, but the relation between A's being a sufficient condition of B and B's being a necessary condition of A, as these relations are ordinarily understood, cannot be interpreted merely on truth-functional grounds. According to the truth-functional interpretation of necessary conditions and sufficient conditions, the following is a logical truth:

(i) A is a sufficient condition of B if and only if B is a necessary condition of A.

But if (i) is supposed to be a (partial) account of our ordinary concept of a necessary condition and a sufficient condition, counterexamples are easy to find. Wertheimer suggests the following examples [1968: 358]: 'Being at least 21 is a necessary condition of being a voter, but it would be absurd to say that being a voter is a (sufficient) condition of being 21'; 'Making a touchdown is a sufficient condition of scoring six points, but it would be absurd to say that scoring six points is a necessary condition of making a touchdown'.

If (i) does not hold, it follows immediately that the following bi-conditional does not hold either:

> (ii) A is a necessary and sufficient condition of B if and only if B is a necessary and sufficient condition of A

In other words, the so-called 'logical bi-conditional' also fails to capture something essential to our natural understanding of NS conditions. Recall the example of Tom: even though Tom's death is a NS condition for his wife Janie's becoming a widow, Janie's becoming a widow is not a NS condition of Tom's death.

On a closer look, there seem to be two things to be distinguished here. One is an *inferential relation*[9], which undeniably is symmetric, between the fact that Tom dies and the fact that his wife Janie becomes a widow—that Janie becomes a widow can be inferred from the fact that Tom dies, as much as the latter can be inferred from the former; The other is a *conditional relation*, which can very well be asymmetric, between Tom's death and Janie's becoming a widow—while Tom's death is a necessary and sufficient condition of Janie's becoming a widow, it can hardly be said that Janie's becoming a widow is a necessary and sufficient condition of his death. By conflating the two relations, a logician may persuade us that from the fact that Tom's death is a *condition* of his wife's becoming a widow, it can be *inferred*, according to the mutual inferential relation between the fact that Tom dies and the fact that his wife

---

[9] Wertheimer calls it 'evidential relation'. While I think 'inferential relation' is better in that it can cover cases in mathematics or logics more transparently, the difference is only terminological.

becomes a widow, that his wife's becoming a widow is also a condition of his death. But this is misleading. Whether the inferential relation is symmetric is one thing, but whether the conditional relation is too is quite another.

In the light of this distinction, it looks as though our foregoing discussion may have failed to do justice to Mill's NS condition analysis. Simply because a two-way inferential relation implied by a NS conditional is symmetric, it does not mean that the NS conditional relation *itself* must therefore be symmetric. By the same token, insofar as INUS conditionality is merely construed as a formal logical relation, we can infer from A's being an INUS condition of B that B is also an INUS condition of A, but from this it does not follow that the INUS conditionality, *qua* conditionality, cannot contain any conditional asymmetry independent of this inferential symmetry.

The lesson we can learn from Wertheimer's discussion is as follows. There is some kind of asymmetry[10] inherent to our natural conception of conditionality

---

[10] I am not sure if a conditional relation can be generally regarded as *asymmetric*, or just *non-symmetric*. If it can be said

that is missed in the formal treatment of conditionality in logic. Generally, a distinction should be made between a formal inferential relation between A and B, and, beyond that, a genuine conditional relation between A and B. Part of this distinction is that there are circumstances in which the inferential relation goes both ways, and yet the conditional relation goes only one way. Inferential relations aside, it may be the case that some kind of asymmetry is involved in conditionality, and therefore be

---

that A&B is a condition of $\neg(\neg A \vee \neg B)$, it can also be said that $\neg(\neg A \vee \neg B)$ is a condition of A&B, and vice versa: the two conditional relations are symmetric. But, if I am right then this kind of restrictive treatment of conditionality in logic is misleading. So the logical example cannot be used to show that a *real* conditional relation can be symmetric. Nevertheless, here is another example: that the earth orbits the sun once can be said to be a condition of one year's passing, but it appears that we can say, with equal plausibility, that one year's passing is also a condition of the earth's orbiting the sun once (of course, whether the conditional relation between the two events ((?)) is a causal one is another question). If the example stands, then it appears that out of the domain of logic there can still be cases in which a conditional relation is symmetric. Therefore, generally speaking, it is safer to say that a condition relation is non-symmetric, rather than always asymmetric.

used to account for causal asymmetry. If this is the case, it appears that Mill's NS conditional analysis or other similar analyses may still stand a chance of being right in accounting for causal asymmetry.

But caution is, again, in order. Insofar as the idea is that conditionality as we naturally understand it has, in some respects, a kind of asymmetry, different from the formal necessary and/or sufficient conditionality. Wertheimer's position is very strong. The problem, however, is to what extent this idea can be useful in developing a theory of causation. The formal necessary and/or sufficient conditionality being suspended, what is left for us to use in constructing a theory of causation in terms of conditionality? It appears that, after making some necessary demarcations among different kinds of condition relations, legal and causal for instance, we can only say something like 'A causes B if and only if A is a causal condition of B.' But, obviously, this is fairly uninformative. No doubt, it is useful, and sometimes vital, to distinguish causal conditions from other kinds of conditions. It can be said that one way of asking for a philosophical theory of causation is just to ask what can serve as a criterion to differentiate causal conditions from other kinds of conditions. But seeking a criterion of *causal conditionality* among different kinds of conditionality is like seeking a criterion of *causal relationship* among different kinds of relationship. As long as we can differentiate causal relations from other kinds of relations, to maintain that a causal relation is also a kind of conditionality would not help (though, not hinder either) to our understanding of causation. Can it make much difference that, if instead of talking about A as the *cause* of B, we talk about A as the *causal condition* of B?

This reveals a general problem with all conditional analyses of causation. In the sense that the causal relationship can be construed as some kind of conditionality, the basic idea of the conditional analysis cannot be wrong, but it is not of much use either. It may be pointed out that, in talking about conditionality we can make use of the notions of a necessary condition and a sufficient condition, which are not readily applicable in talking about relationships in general. It seems that Mill's NS conditional analysis is attractive mainly in that by introducing the formal treatment of necessary and/or sufficient conditions the conditional analysis can be to some extent substantiated. Unfortunately, as we have seen, this practice distorts our concept of conditionality—conditionality as we naturally understand it is in conflict with the formal treatment. Are there, nevertheless, any natural and uncorrupted notions of necessary condition and sufficient condition that we can make use of? Wertheimer's suggestion [1968: 360] is that '[t]he necessary conditions are those conditions such that, if they do not obtain, their consequences do not obtain (or alternatively—cannot obtain). The sufficient conditions are those conditions are those conditions such that, if they obtain, their consequences do obtain (or alternatively—cannot obtain).' But this is just common sense. No doubt, common sense can be important—the significance of Wertheimer's discussion consists precisely in showing how truth-functional conditionality is in conflict with our common sense understanding of conditionality. It is, however, one thing to show what conditionality *is not*, and another to show what it *is*. In order to do the latter, simply appealing to common sense or intuitive examples is not enough. It appears that, without a positive and substantial account of conditionality being supplied, it is hard to see how the conditional analysis can in any significant way contribute to a theory of causation.

Of course, there may still be a chance, however slim, that the conditional analysis can in some way be substantiated. But another problem with the conditional analysis is that it appears that sometimes we need to resort to the notion of causation in order to decide whether a certain relation is of a kind of conditionality, while the inverse relation is not. In maintaining that Tom's death is a condition of Janie's becoming a widow but denying the reverse, the criterion we were tacitly referring to, if I am right, is that while Tom's death causes Janie to become a widow, the opposite is not the case.[11] If we need to, even just occasionally[12], invoke the notion of causation to tell real conditionality from pseudo conditionality, then it should be the case that the notion of causation is at least as basic as conditionality, and attempts to analyze causation in terms of conditionality is in danger of putting the cart before the horse.

Both problems, the problem of being uninformative and the problem of putting the cart before the horse,

---

[11] It may be said that the reason why Tom's death is a condition of his wife's becoming a widow but not the other way around is rather that the former has to occur *before* the latter. But this can't be right. It seems that Tom's wife becomes a widow no sooner or later than he dies.

[12] No doubt, some kinds of conditionality, legal conditionality for example, are non-causal; for this kind of conditionality causal considerations are irrelevant.

undermine attempts to come up with an account of causal asymmetry in terms of conditional asymmetry. If there are no gains in accounting for causation in terms of conditionality, there can hardly be any gains in accounting for causal asymmetry in terms of conditional asymmetry. It may be noted that in talking about the conditional asymmetry in a condition-consequence pair, Wertheimer [1968: 357] suggests, again in a commonsensical way, the following: '[I]f Q is a consequence of P, then Q must be both (I) in some way *posterior* to P and (II) in some way *dependent* on P. Conversely, if P is a condition of Q, then P must be both (I) in some way *prior* to Q and (II) in some way *nondependent* on Q.' Note that I do not here mean to complain that Wertheimer's account is vague (due to his use of the phrase 'in some way'). By this expression Wertheimer means, as he indicates explicitly, that additional work needs to be done in order to spell out the criteria for distinguishing the various types of conditional relations (causal, logical, legal). The point, however, is that even if the differentiations among types of conditional relations can be spelt out, the asymmetries involved in those types of conditional relations—that is, the priorities and dependencies *themselves*—will still remain unexplained. While I agree with Wertheimer [ibid.] that '[t]he kind of priority and dependency is a matter of the type of [conditional] relation involved', it is clear that to know why a conditional relation is of a certain kind and, for that matter why the conditional asymmetry involved is of that kind, is not enough, and not obviously relevant, to knowing why it is asymmetric. In particular, to know why a conditional relation is of a causal kind is not enough (or clearly relevant to) to show why it is (causally) asymmetric.[13] Wertheimer's suggestion, therefore, can at most be regarded as stating, but not explaining, the fact that between a condition and its consequence there is some conditional asymmetry, of which causal asymmetry can be a kind. Since, as I have argued, the notion of a causal condition and that of a causal relation are on the same conceptual level, it appears that to differentiate causal-condition asymmetry from other kinds of conditional asymmetry will be no more and no less than to differentiate causal-relational asymmetry—that is, what we

---

[13] Unless, of course, the causal conditionality or relationship is simply *defined* as being asymmetric. But, as I argued in the Introduction, causal asymmetry should better not be established in this cheap way.

normally mean by 'causal asymmetry'—from other kinds of relational asymmetries.

What makes the situation even more hopeless is that it seems that sometimes we need to resort to the notion of causal asymmetry in order to tell whether a certain conditionality in question is asymmetric at all. Actually, I think that an important reason why those conditional symmetry theses (the stipulated symmetry in NS conditionality for example) that result from the formal treatment of necessary and/or sufficient conditions look plausible is that in logic we always assume that causal factors should not be taken into account. It appears to be the case that it is only when we begin to consider causal factors that we realize that there is a discrepancy between our natural understanding of conditionality and the formal treatment of it; and it is only when we begin to notice some causal asymmetry that some conditional asymmetry comes into light.

To conclude, I have argued in the last two sections that the regularity theory including the various forms of conditional analyses of causation, contributes very little to our understanding of causal asymmetry. That there is no asymmetric element to be discovered in those typical conditional analyses, analyses that more or less appeal to the formal treatment of necessary and/or sufficient conditions, is only to be expected. Conditionality as we commonly understand it does contain in itself some kind of asymmetry. It has been shown to be futile, however, to analyze causal asymmetry in terms of the kind of asymmetry we sense in conditional asymmetry, just as it is futile to analyze causation in terms of conditionality at large. In a broad, and trivial, sense, whatever can be said about causal asymmetry can be said about causal-condition asymmetry as well; but this by itself is not a merit of the conditional analysis, but rather an indication of its inability to account for causal asymmetry.

Chapter 2

Causal Asymmetry and Causal Forks

2.1 Introduction

2.2 The Basic Analysis: Hausman

2.3 Improvement I: Ehring

2.4 Improvement II: Lewis

2.1 Introduction

Often we start discussing causation by focusing on a single causal relation in the form of 'A causes B', in which A and B are both supposed to be single causal factor, say events. But arguably the idea of a single causal relation in this form is an ideal, in the sense that in reality causal relata are more likely than not to be *multiple*.[14] Instead of 'A causes B', what we usually have is a causal relation in the form of '(A, C, and E ...) causes (B, D, and F ...)', in which distinct event A, C, and E ... jointly cause distinct event B, D, and F.... In the simplest form of multiple causes, two distinct events join together to cause a third event, e.g., the movement of one billiard ball and the movement of another caused a collision; and in the simplest form of multiple effects, an event causes two other distinct events, not successively—that is, it is not the case that the cause event gives rise to the first effect event, which in turn gives rise to the second—but respectively[15], e.g., an electronic discharge caused lightning and thunder.

---

[14] It is arguable, since perhaps the so-called multiple causes (multiple effects as well) can altogether be regarded as a single 'big' event. If so, the form 'A causes B' is just real. This being said, it may be raised again that this way of individuation of events is only ideal, or worse, simply arbitrary and likely to be wrong.

[15] The two effect events need not occur simultaneously, even though presumably they can. The simultaneity is not required for the branching structure.

These are what we call 'causal forks', which according to their characteristic structures can be classified into two kinds: the fork constituted by a common cause and two or more joint effects (call it 'the common-cause fork'; see Figure 1.1), and the fork constituted by a common effect and two or more joint causes (call it 'the common-effect fork'; see Figure 1.2).[16] It is easy to see that two simple forks can connect to each other and form a compound structure[17], and that a couple

---

[16] Two notes: First, the common-effect fork is different from a structure involving what we usually call 'causal overdetermination', in which each individual cause event is by itself sufficient for the effect event, such as two gunmen simultaneously shot the victim to death. Second, the two forks I am interested here are constituted by *particular* and *occurrent* events, not general ones. Regarding general events, talk of 'the conjunctive fork' is in place (see Reichenbach [1956] and Salmon [1980]), such as in 'smoking causes cancer and yellow fingers'. In this chapter we are not concerned with the conjunctive fork, an adequate characterization of which can only be given by reference to certain statistical considerations.

[17] A common cause in a fork can be one of the joint effects in another; a common effect in a fork can be one of the joint causes in another; a common effect in a fork can be a common cause in another; and a joint effect in a fork can be one of the joint causes in another.

of simple forks can connect to one another and form a causal network. These complexities aside, it seems right to say that the common-cause fork and the common-effect fork are basic fork structures.

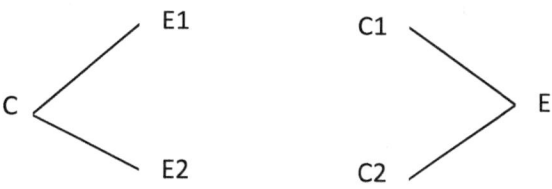

1.1 The Common-Cause Fork   1.2 The Common-Effect Fork

Figure 1: Causal Forks

Since Reichenbach's seminal work [1956][18], many philosophers have discussed causal forks for different

---

[18] His focused on statistically characterized conjunctive forks. But some basic ideas about causal forks in general were already touched upon.

purposes.[19] The area as I see it is, though productive, messy and obscure. We need to explore this area though, because one of the most significant consequences of the study of causal forks is often claimed to be that a certain kind of fork asymmetry is responsible for causal asymmetry, or the cause-effect distinction.

But for our limited purpose not every issue about causal forks needs to be addressed. In particular, the temporal relations involved in causal forks are not our concern. Some philosophers, Reichenbach and Horwich for example, discuss fork structures mainly with the aim to find out some kind of fork asymmetry on which the asymmetry of *time* is built; but they are not particularly interested in the causal structure of the forks.[20] In the Introduction I pointed out that the problem of causal asymmetry is different from, and could very well be independent of, the problem of temporal asymmetry between cause and effect. It is true that, as a matter of

---

[19] See, for example, Lewis [1979], Salmon [1980], Ehring [1982], Hausman [1984], Papineau [1985, 1992], and Horwich [1987].

[20] To discuss their projects in any detail would take us too far afield. For those who are interested, see Reichenbach [1956: Ch. 4, Sect. 19], and Horwich [1987: Ch. 4, Sect. 8, and Ch. 8, Sect. 1].

fact, the joint effects in a common-cause fork are usually later than the common cause; and the joint causes in a common-effect fork are usually earlier than the common effect. Thus, in Figure 1, if we supply an 'arrow' of time that points from the left (the past) to the right (the future), it can be said that usually a common-cause fork is open to the future whereas a common-effect fork is open to the past. However, from this it does not follow that the temporal-opening structures are necessarily associated with the causal-branching structures. While I have nothing substantial to add to what I have already said in the Introduction about the general distinction between causal asymmetry and temporal asymmetry between cause and effect, it suffices here to point out that, for example, in cases of simultaneous causation the temporal-opening structures perishes but the causal-branching structures remain intact, and that in cases of backwards causation, which at any rate we do not want to rule out a priori, a causal fork even opens against its normal temporal direction. At any rate, nothing I argue in this chapter will hinge upon temporal relations involved in causal forks.

On the other hand, I am aware that according to the so-called 'causal theory of time' it may be that asymmetry *of* time (the earlier-later distinction) is reducible to causal asymmetry (the cause-effect distinction). Although in my view this is wrong, I won't say anything against it. As long as a friend of the causal theory of time holds that causal asymmetry is by no means reducible to the temporal asymmetry between cause and effect, I have no problem with it. I will in this chapter content myself to evaluate some major attempts to make use of fork asymmetry to account for causal asymmetry, leaving the question whether the latter can be further employed in accounting for the asymmetry of time, a question that is independent of the first, undecided.

2.2 The Basic Analysis: Hausman

Daniel Hausman [1984][21] argues that causal asymmetry consists in a certain structural feature of causal forks. Since his analysis contains some basic ideas needed in our later discussion, it is convenient to start with him. Here is Hausman's official analysis [265]:

---

[21] Henceforth all references made to Hausman are from this work.

X causes Y[22] if and only if

(1) X is causally connected to Y,

(2) everything causally connected to X is causally connected to Y, and

(3) something is causally connected to Y, but not to X.

Note first that, despite appearance, this analysis is not an analysis of *causation*. (Were it an analysis of causation, it would be crudely circular, since the notion of *causal* connection is mentioned explicitly in the analysans.) Rather, it is meant to be an analysis of *causal asymmetry*, or the distinction between cause and effect. In other words, the aim of this analysis is to decide, as between

---

[22] X and Y are either particular events, or particular states of affairs. Hausman's analysis draws no distinction between events and states with respect to their causal status [261]. We will follow this understanding throughout this chapter. For simplicity, we will only speak about events.

two causally connected events X and Y, which is the cause and which is the effect. To carry out such an analysis, Hausman assumes the notion of causal connection as primitive. According to him, two events can be asserted to be causally connected without that assertion entailing which is the cause and which is the effect. Provided this assumption, I agree that his analysis cannot be rejected simply on the ground that, since every causal connection is *ipso facto* causally asymmetric, to analyze causal asymmetry by making use of the notion of causal connection is circular.

What, then, is it for X and Y to be causally connected? According to Hausman's definition [263], X is causally connected to Y, just in case (a) X causes Y, or (b) Y causes X, or (c) X and Y have a common cause. This definition is very important, both to his analysis of causal asymmetry and my criticism of it. I will return to it shortly.

The following example shows how Hausman's analysis is supposed to work. My striking of a match caused its lighting, but it is not the case that the lighting caused the striking. This is so, according to Hausman's analysis, because everything causally connected to the striking of the match, for instance my possessing of the match, is also causally connected to the lighting; by contrast, something causally connected to the lighting, for instance the presence of oxygen, is not causally connected to the striking. For a better diagnosis, consider this illustration of the example:

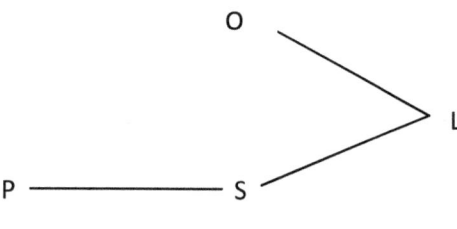

Figure 2

In the figure, 'P' stands for the possessing of the match, 'S' for the striking, 'O' for the presence of oxygen, and 'L' for the lighting. Hausman's idea, to restate it with these symbols, is that P, which is causally connected to S, is also causally connected to L, whereas O, which is causally connect to L, is not causally connected to S. Suppose, for reasons to be discussed shortly, that everything causally connected to S is also causally connected to L (for instance P is), and that something causally connected to L is nevertheless not causally connected to S (for instance O isn't), then, according to Hausman's analysis, S causes L, which is also to say that the causal asymmetry obtains between L and F.

That there is something causally connected to L but not to S is obvious, for O is such a thing. The reason we suppose that *everything* causally connected to S is also causally connected to L, on the other hand, appears to be this. To start with, P, which is a cause of S, is causally connected to L (by way of S). So presumably all events that stand on the *cause-side* of S are causally connected to F. Now, how about events standing on the *effect-side* of S? Suppose that the lighting caused by my striking of the match in turn caused a fire (F). Then what happened is like this:

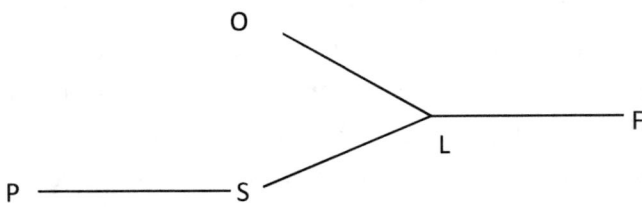

Figure 3

In this case, F, which is an effect of S (by way of L), is of course also causally connected to L. So presumably all events that stand on the effect-side of S are also causally connected to L as well. Now, if events both on the cause-side and on the effect-side of S are all causally connected to L, it appears right to say that everything causally connected to S is also causally connected to L. Obviously, this is in accord with clause (2) in Hausman's analysis.

Now, while some far-fetched counterexamples can be created to shed doubt on Hausman's analysis, I won't count on this kind of criticism. So even if it can be said that by the Big Bang everything in the world is directly or indirectly causally connected (if this is so then Hausman's analysis is apparently problematic, because clause (3) cannot be satisfied), Hausman's response to this objection [266], namely that it is good enough if his analysis works just for *local* causal asymmetries, seems reasonable. Moreover, it may be said that in a 'simple world', a world in which, say, only two small particles exist and one hits another, Hausman's analysis will fail to apply, for the obvious reason that in such a world we cannot find a third causal factor needed for clause (2) and (3) in his analysis to apply. To this objection Hausman might say that in such a simple world there would be no causation, and for that matter no causal asymmetry either. If this sounds too strong he might say instead that in such a world the causal asymmetry of the hitting is established by *projecting* onto this world our usual notion of causal asymmetry, which rests on our observation of what happens in the more complex actual world. Granted, how this projection works exactly can be a problem. But, as was said, let's set aside these highly unrealistic counter-examples and their possible defenses.

A crucial problem in Hausman's analysis, however, is with the central notion of his analysis: causal connection. Note that the lighting example at present only involves a fork structure of a kind that I have called the common-effect fork, in which the two joint causes, O and S, cause L. But, instead of merely being a joint cause of L, S can also be a common cause in another fork, of a kind that I have called the common-cause fork. In the example, it appears reasonable to suppose that, besides jointly causing the lighting, my striking of the match may also have caused some other effect events, for instance a scratching sound (S'). If so, what happened can be illustrated as:

Causal Asymmetry and Causal Forks

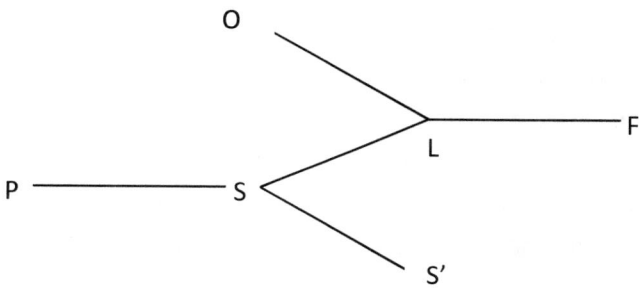

Figure 4

What would Hausman have to say about the causal relations between S' and other events in the example? Obviously, in order to uphold clause (2) in his formulation, (i.e., that everything causally connected to the cause, in this case S, is causally connected to the effect, in this case L), he has to maintain that S', which is apparently causally connected to S, is also causally connected to L. He does maintain this, *by fiat*. According to his definition of causal connection (which we mentioned two pages ago), when S' and F have a common cause, they are just regarded as causally connected. But for what *reason* should we accept this? The question becomes acute when it is noticed that, according to his definition, in the common-effect fork O-L-S, the two joint causes, O and S, are not causally connected, whereas in the common-cause fork L-S-S', the two joint effects, L and S', are nevertheless causally connected. But why is there this differentiation, such that joint effects are causally connected whereas joint causes are not?

I can think of two reasons that might have led Hausman to make this differentiation; both are problematic. First, it is true that, given certain circumstances and laws of nature, in the common-cause fork the common cause is sufficient for both of the joint effects. In other words, the co-occurrence of the joint effects (if they occur at all) is nomically necessitated by the common cause. In contrast, it appears that the co-occurrence of the joint causes in a common-effect fork is not nomically necessary—in the example, there appear to be no laws of nature dictating that my scratching of the match has to occur together with the presence of oxygen. If so, can this difference with regard to nomic necessity between the co-occurrence of joint effects and that of joint causes justify Hausman's definition of joint effects as causally connected and joint causes as not? It would appear not. For one thing, there is a clear conceptual difference between *nomically necessary co-occurrence* on one hand, and *causal connection* on the other. For another, the two concepts may not even be co-extensive. In cases of chance events at least, it seems that we can have causal connections that are not nomically necessary. So even though presumably my tossing a coin is causally connected with its showing heads, it is at least doubtful whether the two events' co-occurrence is a nomic necessity.[23]

Second, it may be that in a sense joint effects are more *statistically* connected than joint causes. Suppose that $P(L\&S') > P(L) \times P(S')$[24], as it appears so, then it may be felt that L and S' are connected to a degree that O and S aren't. Regarding O and S, which are joint causes,

---

[23] By 'co-occurrence' I do not mean two occurrences *at the same time*; obviously the tossing of the coin and its showing head do not occur at the same time. But neither do the scratching sound and the lighting. I use 'co-occurrence' in a loose sense that the two events in question occur *together*.

[24] Roughly, this is to say that the lighting and the scratching sound occur together more frequently than they would if they were statistically independent of one another.

it is more likely to be the case that $P(O\&S) = P(O) \times P(S)$[25]. So in this sense there is a contrast in terms of the statistical association among joint causes and that among joint effects and Hausman's intuition that joint effects are causally connected whereas joint causes are not may be based on this contrast. But the notion of causal connection as we commonly understand it is distant from the notion of statistical correlation. Hausman's endorsement of the causal connection among joint effects but denial of the causal connection among joint causes, if actually backed by statistical considerations, is without further ado unjustified. However, when he does discuss statistical considerations [p. 269], his opinion is that the statistical features associated with causal asymmetry are only evidential, and are only significant in testing a certain causal asymmetry that is already there.

As far as I can see, there seems to be no good reason to endorse Hausman's definition of causal connection in saying that joint effects are causally connected but joint causes are not. It appears that his conception of causal

---

[25] Roughly, this is to say that the presence of oxygen and the scratching of the match occur together equally frequently as they do when they are statistically independent of one another.

connection is just a matter of preference—as he puts it, a 'conviction' [263]. But this conception seems quite ad hoc—it is hard to see what, other than suiting the purpose of his analysis of causal asymmetry, the point of the conception is. I conclude therefore that Hausman's analysis of causal asymmetry, which hinges upon this peculiar conception of causal connection, is unconvincing.

2.3 Improvement I: Ehring

Like Hausman, Douglas Ehring [1982] [26] also takes the notion of causal connection as basic to his analysis of causal asymmetry in terms of fork asymmetry. But—importantly—unlike Hausman, when Ehring says 'c is causally connected to e' he only means that either c causes e or e causes c [767-8] [27]. In other words, Ehring only allows causal connections *in a direct line*, and does

---

[26] Henceforth all references made to Ehring are from this work.

[27] Ehring uses small letters to represent particular events or states; for convenience, in formulating his views I follow his usage.

not regard joint effects in a common-cause fork as causally connected. This conception of causal connection is apparently more plausible than Hausman's. Since Ehring bases his analysis of causal asymmetry on this bona fide conception of causal connection, it will not be subject to the objection we raised against Hausman's analysis, and deserve a different treatment.

But Ehring's more plausible conception of causal connection has a price to pay. To see why, note that, again like Hausman, Ehring's analysis of causal asymmetry also consists in saying that, roughly, *while there are certain things causally connected to the effect e but not to the cause c, there is no such thing causally connected to c but not to e.* [770] It seems, then, that Ehring will face an immediate difficulty in case of a common-cause fork in which c is the common cause and e is one of the joint effects. According to his conception of causal connection, the joint effects are all causally connected to c, but not causally connected to each other. It appears that all the joint effects (except perhaps e itself[28]), which are all causally connected to c but not to e, will become straight-

---

[28] This is so, because presumably an event cannot be said as causally connected to itself.

forward counterexamples to his basic thesis that there is no such thing that is causally connected to the cause but not to the effect.

But Ehring designs a maneuver to deal with this difficulty. In order to see how the maneuver works, let's first note that, instead of clause (2) and (3) in Hausman's formulation (i.e., that everything causally connected to c is causally connected to e, and that something is causally connected to e but not to c), the crucial clause in Ehring's analysis of causal asymmetry is:

> There is some *condition* of the causal connection between c and e which is not connected causally to c and is causally connected to e, and there is no *condition* causally connected to c but not to e. [770, italics mine]

So Ehring does not talk about *things* in general, but only his specially defined *conditions*. What is a condition as he understands it? According to him,

> f is a condition of the causal connection between c and e if and only if f is an event or state upon which the causal connection between c and e is counterfactually dependent. [766]

Call this definition *the basic definition of a condition*. It is easy to see that according to this definition, causes of c and joint causes of e are all conditions of the causal connection between c and e.[29] This is because, given the circumstances and the laws of nature, if any cause of c or any joint cause of e had not occurred, the causal connection between c and e would not have been realized. It is important to point out, however, that this definition by itself cannot exclude *joint effects* from counting as conditions of the causal connection between c and e. Suppose that c caused e' as well as e, and that, given the circumstances and the laws of nature, c *could not* fail to cause e'. According to the basic definition of a condition, Ehring has to allow e'

---

[29] c itself is also a condition of the causal connection between c and e, since, obviously, if c had not occurred, the causal connection between c and e would not have been realized.

as a condition of the causal connection between c and e, because the connection is counterfactually dependent on e'—if e' had not occurred, c would not have occurred (and thus c and e would not have been causally connected).

To rule out e' as a condition of the causal connection between c and e, Ehring [p. 767-8] works out a subtle modification to his basic definition of a condition.[30] The

---

[30] It should be mentioned in passing that, in order to deal with the problem of causal pre-emption, Ehring also works out another modification to his basic definition of a condition. Suppose that some back-up conditions which in the absence of f will play the role occupied by f. If so, we cannot say without any qualification that if f had not occurred, the causal connection between c and e would not have been realized. To deal with this problem, Ehring reformulates his definition of condition as follows: f is a condition of the causal connection between c and e if and only if "f is a member of a set of events each of which occurred, such that the causal connection between c and e is counterfactually dependent upon each member in the absence of the other members, where this set includes all and only nonredundant members" [767]. The problem of causal pre-emption, as I see it, is not a serious one for Ehring's definition of condition, and I assume his treatment of the problem is adequate. In the following I will disregard the

basic idea of his modification, as far as I can tell, is this. Suppose that, besides c, there is another event, for example g, which contributed in jointly causing e'.[31] This supposition seems to be reasonable—after all, it is unlikely that c is the sole cause of e'. Now, in the presence of g, c alone will cease to be sufficient for e', and thus c (and the causal connection between c and e) will cease to be counterfactually dependent on e'. For, in a case in which e' had not occurred, it is not necessarily the case that c would not have occurred—*c could still have occurred, if it is stipulated rather that g might have failed to occur, and thus the absence of e' might have been rendered by the absence of g instead*. Consequently, if c (and the causal connection between c and e) is not counterfactually dependent on e', then, according to the basic definition of a condition, e' is not a condition of the causal connection between c and e. By contrast, it appears that for f—no matter if it is a cause of c, or one of the joint causes of e—on which the causal connection

---

problem and Ehring's treatment of it; otherwise the discussion will become too cumbersome.

[31] Note that in supposing this we are supposing some new circumstances, different from the original circumstances which made c alone sufficient for e'.

Causal Asymmetry and Causal Forks

between c and e is counterfactually dependent and which according to the basic definition of a condition is also a condition of that connection, the situation is quite different. It appears that to introduce an extra event will in no way stop the causal connection between c and e being counterfactually dependent on f. If so, then we can define a genuine condition of the causal connection between c and e, namely f, as an event on which the causal connection between c and e is counterfactual dependent, and, *as a proviso*, there being no event on which f counterfactually depends the stipulated presence of which would make the causal connection between c and e cease to be counterfactually dependent on f. By contrast, a 'fake' condition, namely e', is an event on which the causal connection between c and e is counterfactually dependent, but there are some events on which e' is counterfactually dependent the stipulated presence of which would make the causal connection between c and e cease to be counterfactually dependent on e'. If this contrast between f and e' is correct, then it seems that Ehring can retain the right sort of conditions (i.e., events like f, no matter whether they are causes of c, or joint causes of e) needed in his analysis of causal asymmetry, and at the same time get rid of unwanted 'conditions' (i.e., events like e', joint effects of c).

Ehring's discussion is abstract, and he didn't use any substantive and detailed example to show how his maneuver is supposed to work, or so I read. I shall then try to clarify his idea, as charitable as I can, by extending the lighting example introduced earlier. My striking of the match caused the match's lighting and the scratching sound. Obviously, according to Ehring's conception of a causal connection (i.e., two events are causally connected just in case either of them causes the other), the scratching sound is causally connected to the striking but not to the lighting. Moreover, according to his basic definition of a condition (i.e., f is a condition of the causal connection between c and e if and only if f is an event upon which the causal connection between c and e is counterfactually dependent), the scratching sound should be regarded as a condition of the causal connection between the striking and the lighting, because, given the circumstances and the laws of nature, if the scratching sound had not occurred, the striking would not have occurred, and as a result the causal connection between the striking and the lighting would also not have obtained. The problem, however, is that Ehring cannot allow the scratching sound to be counted as a condition of the causal connection between the striking and the lighting, since otherwise the scratching sound would constitute a counterexample to the central clause in his analysis of causal asymmetry, namely 'there is some condition of the causal connection between c and e which is not connected causally to c and is causally connected to e, and there is no condition causally connected to c but not to e'. Against this clause, were the scratching sound a condition of the causal connection between the striking and the lighting, it would be just a condition causally connected to the striking but not to the lighting.

Now, Ehring needs a maneuver by which he can rule out the scratching sound, a joint effect with the lighting, as a condition of the causal connection between the striking and the lighting. And his maneuver is this: Presumably, there are some events other than the striking of the match, such as the presence of air through which the scratching sound-wave travelled, that also contributed in causing the scratching sound. If so, the striking will cease to be sufficient for the scratching sound; and it follows that the causal connection between the striking and the lighting will cease to be counterfactually dependent on the scratching sound. In other words, given the laws of nature and the *new* circumstances in which the presence of air is introduced, it is not anymore the case that if the scratching sound had not occurred (this might have been due to the absence of air) then the striking would not have occurred (and thus would not have caused the lighting).

(Note—this is a little twist—that, for the example to work, by 'air' we have to mean some gases other than oxygen. If we stipulate that air *as we normally understand it* is absent and, as a result, the oxygen in it is also absent, then the lighting, which requires oxygen, would not have occurred and thus the causal connection between the striking and the lighting would not have obtained. Consequently, the causal connection between the striking and the lighting would still be counterfactually dependent, via the stipulation of the absence of air and for that matter the stipulation of the absence of oxygen, on the scratching sound.[32])

---

[32] To avoid confusion, it may be better to choose to introduce another cause of the scratching sound, in a way such that it is explicitly distinct from the presence of oxygen and any other genuine conditions of the causal connection between the striking and the lighting. But I find it's hard come up with a

Causal Asymmetry and Causal Forks

By contrast, the presence of oxygen, unlike the presence of air in the way we understand it in the example, is a genuine condition of the causal connection between the striking and the lighting. It is so, because no matter what event is introduced into the scenario, it appears that the causal connection between the striking and the lighting will all the same be counterfactually dependent on the presence of oxygen. Or, in other words, the counterfactual, 'If oxygen had not been present, the striking of the match would not have caused the lighting', will always be true.

In a nutshell, the maneuver Ehring comes up with to fend off the scratching sound as a condition of the causal connection between the striking and the lighting is this: By introducing a cause of the scratching sound, for instance the presence of air, the counterfactual dependence of the causal connection between the striking and the

---

nice cause of this kind. Maybe *all creatures' hearing ability* will do. But for obvious reasons to take the (?) ability as a cause of the scratching sound will bring into the example under discussion unnecessary controversies; and the phrasing of the cause sounds awkward anyway. So I decide to stay with my choice of 'the presence of air', with the caution in mind that the 'air' here refers to some non-oxygen gases.

lighting on the scratching sound will cease to hold; by contrast, it seems that there is no cause of the presence of oxygen—actually, no event whatsoever—the introduction of which will undermine the counterfactual dependence of the causal connection between the striking and the lighting on the presence of oxygen. Taking this contrast into consideration, we can therefore work out a general proviso to the basic definition of a condition (as we saw two pages ago), so as to reject the scratching or the like, but to retain the presence of oxygen or the like, as a genuine condition of the causal connection between the striking and the lighting.

This contrast, however, is an illusion. To see this, first notice that a crucial move in Ehring's construction of this contrast is to argue that, in the example set out, once one takes into consideration of the presence of air the striking of the match will no longer appear to be counterfactually dependent on the scratching sound. To unpack his rationale behind this argument, let's say that once the presence of air is introduced the striking of the match will cease to be *sufficient* for the scratching sound [768], which presumably is also to say that the scratching sound will cease to be *necessary* for the striking[33]. And if the scratching sound is not necessary for the striking, it in turn follows that the striking is not counterfactually dependent on the scratching sound.

It seems, however, that by the same rationale it can be argued that the causal connection between the striking and the lighting will also fail to be counterfactually dependent on what Ehring has taken to be *genuine* conditions of the causal connection, for example the presence of oxygen or the striking of the match. If so, his intended contrast between genuine and 'fake' conditions of the causal connection collapses.

Let me explain with Figure 5. In this figure, 'A' stands for the presence of air, 'B' for my breathing as an joint effect (with the lighting of the match) of the presence of oxygen, other symbols for what they stand before (i.e., 'O' for the presence of oxygen, 'L' for the lighting of the match, 'S' for my striking of the match, and 'S'' for the scratching sound); causal factors irrele-

---

[33] As we have seen in Ch. 1.2, this is not so easy. The question whether c's being sufficient for e entails e's being necessary for c is generally not so easy. But my criticism of Ehring's manoeuvre does not point to this question. Let's for the sake of argument grant that c is sufficient for e if and only if e is necessary for c.

vant to our present purpose, such as causes of S and effects of L, are neglected.

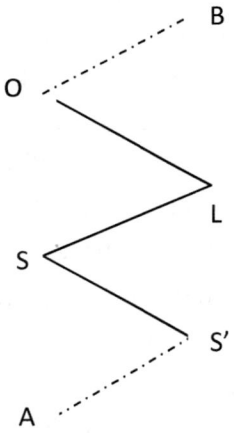

Figure 5

Ehring's point is that, as a result of the introduction of an extra event A, we have a common-effect fork, S-S'-A. In this common-effect fork, S is not sufficient for S', and thus S' is not necessary for S, and thus S is not counterfactually dependent on S', and thus the causal connection between S and L is not counterfactually dependent on S'. According to his basic definition of a condition, this means in turn that S' is not a condition of the causal connection between S and L. On the other hand, O is regarded as a condition of the causal connection between S and L[34], because, it is said, the causal connection is counterfactually dependent on O. But why, by introducing an extra event B and thus *with regard to the common-cause fork, L-S-S'*, one cannot argue—for the above same reason Ehring argues that the causal connection between S and L is not counterfactually dependent on S'—that, since O is not necessary for L, and thus L is not counterfactually dependent on O, and thus the causal connection between S and L is not counterfactually dependent on O?

In reply to this question, Ehring may quickly point out that, against our supposition, O must be necessary for L, since O is only one of the two joint causes (O and S) of L. But this will not do. Note in saying that O is necessary

---

[34] Ehring also regards S as a condition of the causal connection between S and L. What I argue in the follows, *mutatis mutandis*, can also be argued about O.

for L what we mean is that as far as the common-effect fork O-L-S is concerned, O as a joint cause is necessary for the common effect L. But, similarly, it can also be said that, as far as the common-cause fork L-S-S' is concerned, S' must be necessary for S. If so, it follows that, notwithstanding the introduction of A, S (and thus the causal connection between S and L) must be counter-factually dependent on S', and thus S' must be, contra Ehring's original reasoning, a genuine condition of the causal connection between S and L. Now, either we adopt Ehring's original reasoning, so as to say that O and S' are both necessary for, and for that matter are both conditions of, the causal connection between S and L, or we adopt the reason employed in his reply, so as to say that O and S' are both not necessary for, and for that matter are both not condition of, the causal connection between S and L. Either way, his intended contrast between O and S' does not exist.

Understandably, it may be objected that the crucial point here is that the common-effect fork O-L-S is *dissimilar* to the common-cause fork L-S-S', in that with regard to the former fork either of the two joint causes, O and S, can be said to be necessary for the common effect L, whereas with regard to the later fork neither of the two joint effects, L and S', can be said to be necessary for the common cause S. I agree. But the problem for Ehring is that there appear to be no conceptual resources at his disposal to make sense of this dissimilarity. Obviously, he is not in a position to say that the dissimilarity consists in the fact that O and S are *causes* whereas L and S' are *effects*, and that only causes can be meaningfully said to be necessary/sufficient for their effects but not the other way around.[35] The distinction between cause and effect is what he is trying to analyze, so he cannot make use of this distinction in his analysis, on pain of circularity. Alternatively, it may be suggested that the distinct temporal structures of these two forks can be used to account for the required dissimilarity. But Ehring [761] explicitly claims that temporal structures of causal forks are not our

---

[35] This is my favourite line of approach. My view is that without first making sense of causal asymmetry we cannot make sense of necessary/sufficient conditions in which events are involved (this has been to some extent discussed in Ch. 1.2), and that without first making sense of causal asymmetry in causal connections (in Ehring's sense) we cannot make sense of fork asymmetry. In my view, to analyze causal asymmetry in terms of fork asymmetry is to put the cart before the horse.

concern in analyzing causal asymmetry (which has, in any case, been a continual presupposition of this chapter).

As a final attempt, it may be suggested that we can get around issues associated with necessary/sufficient dependences in causal forks altogether, and simply talk about counterfactual dependences in these forks. Anyway, Ehring's defines his notion of condition in terms of counterfactual dependence, not in terms of necessary/sufficient dependence. So for example in the common-effect fork O-L-S, regardless whether O qualifies as necessary for L, the counterfactual, 'If O had not occurred, L would not have occurred (and thus the causal connection between S and L would not have obtained)', is intuitively right; whereas in the common-effect fork L-S-S', regardless whether S' can be said to be necessary for S, the counterfactual, 'If S' had not occurred, S would not have occurred (and thus the causal connection between S and L would not have obtained)', is intuitively wrong. Put generally, the point is that in a common-effect fork the common effect is counterfactually dependent on each and every joint cause, whereas in a common-cause fork the common cause is not counterfactually dependent on any of the joint causes.

This, however, is to return to the problem Ehring started with. The reason he introduced an extra joint cause such as A to construct the common-effect fork S-S'-A, with the help of the notion of necessary/sufficient dependence, is precisely to explain *why* the counterfactual, 'If S' has not occurred, S would not have occurred (and thus the causal connection between S and L would not have obtained)', is wrong. Now, if we take the judgment to be merely intuitive, no problem then needs to be solved in the first place. But a counterfactual of that sort, we can agree with Ehring, is wrong for a reason; and its wrongness needs to be explained. It is only that Ehring has failed to provide such a reason.

2.4 Improvement II: Lewis

We have seen that Ehring's maneuver is unsuccessful in ruling out a joint effect e' from counting as a genuine condition of c, and thus as a genuine condition of the causal connection between c and e. Note that what Ehring needs here, in effect, is an argument to show that a cause is not counterfactually dependent on its effect. This readily reminds us Lewis' well-known thesis that an effect is counterfactually dependent on its cause, in a way that the cause is not counterfactually dependent on the effect. If Lewis' thesis is defendable, it can be applied to Ehring's definition of condition, and thereby save the latter's analysis of causal asymmetry.[36] Actually, Hausman or Ehring's work aside, Lewis' analysis of counterfactual asymmetry has a direct bearing on the notion of causal asymmetry. For, according to his analysis, E is causally dependent on C (but not the other way around) if and only if E is counterfactually dependent on C (but not the other way around). So our discussion of causal asymmetry is incomplete without an evaluation of Lewis' work.

To start with, a few words need to be said about the background of Lewis' work. Lewis advocates a counter-

---

[36] Lewis discussed counterfactual asymmetry in two papers: first briefly in [1973], and then intensively in [1979]. Although Ehring's paper was published shortly after Lewis' 1979 paper, it may be that in writing his paper Ehring didn't study Lewis' work carefully, and therefore didn't mention it, let alone make use of it. Hausman, who published his paper even later, said in a note that he 'had opportunity' to study Lewis' paper during his writing.

factual theory of causation. His counterfactual theory consists in saying, roughly, that for any two actual particular events C and E, E causally depends on C if and only if E counterfactually depends on C, or in other words that if C had not occurred, E would not have occurred.[37] On the face of it, however, there is a problem for this theory. Suppose that C causes E but E does not cause C— in other words, there is no such thing as causally mutual dependence or a causal loop between C and E. And suppose further that, as appears plausible, given the circumstances and the laws of nature, C could not have failed to cause E. It seems then that we can say as well that if E had not occurred, C would not have occurred.[38]

---

[37] The counterfactual theory of causation makes a distinction between causal dependence and causation. While counterfactual dependence is both necessary and sufficient for causal dependence, it is only sufficient but not necessary for causation (which involves causal transitivity). Causation can be analyzed, roughly, by saying that C causes E if and only there is a chain of causal dependences, which in turn are accounted for by a series of counterfactual dependences, starting from C and ending at E.

[38] As we have seen, Ehring faces exactly the same problem when he considers *c* taken to be counterfactually dependent on *e'*.

If so, then, according to the counterfactual theory, E is a cause of C. This, however, contradicts our supposition that E did not cause C.

Lewis calls the above argument that purports to show that a cause C is counterfactually dependent on its effect E a *back-tracking argument* [1979: 476]. Under the framework of the counterfactual theory, Lewis need to show the back-tracking argument to be false, by arguing that it is not the case that if E had not occurred, C would have failed to occur. To see how he tries to do this, we need to have some basic idea of his semantics of counterfactuals:

> A counterfactual 'If it were that A, then it would be that C[39]' is (non-vacuously) true if and only if some (accessible) world where both A and C are true is more similar to our actual world, overall, than is any world where A is true but C is false. [1979: 465]

---

[39] In this quotation 'A' and 'C' are used as dummy sentences asserting the occurrence of events; this is different from my using them as dummy names of events.

To put it simply and to use the familiar symbols, the idea is that the counterfactual 'If C had not occurred then E would not have occurred' is true, if and only if some possible world in which both the antecedent and the consequent are true is more similar to the actual world than any possible world in which the antecedent is true but the consequent is false. Consequently, the counterfactual 'If E had not occurred then C would not have occurred' is false, just in case some possible world in which the antecedent is true but the consequent is false is more similar to the actual world than any possible world in which both the antecedent and the consequent are true.

Apparently, what is crucial to Lewis' semantics of counterfactuals is the notion of a possible worlds' *similarity* to the actual world. For our purpose, it is important to note that the similarity is meant to be an overall one. If we only consider the particular fact of the occurrence of C and that of the occurrence of E, then of course a possible world in which C does not occur but E does is more similar to the actual world (in which C and E both occur) than another possible world in which C and E both do not occur. But from this it does not follow that the first possible world must be *overall* more similar to the actual world than the second. For, if we stipulate C and E do not occur in a possible world, *certain other things in the possible world will also have to be stipulated together with the non-occurrence of C and E*. It is all these things together, not merely the non-occurrence of C and E itself, that make the possible world more (or less) similar to the actual world than another possible world in which E occurs, but as a result some other things will also have to be stipulated to agree with the occurrence of E.

What, then, are the kinds of things we need to consider in order to decide which of two possible worlds is overall more similar to our actual world than the other? Lewis [1979: 472] suggests the following guidelines:

(1) It is of the first importance to avoid big, widespread, diverse violations of law.

(2) It is of the second importance to maximize the spatiotemporal region throughout which perfect match of particular fact prevails.

(3) It is of the third importance to avoid even small, localized, simple violations of law.

(4) It is of little or no importance to secure approximate similarity of particular fact, even in matters that concern us greatly.

Basically, the idea is that in comparison between two possible words (with respect to their similarity to the actual world), the matching of laws of nature weighs much more than the matching of particular facts, even though some minor violation of laws may be less of a departure from the actual world than a massive absence of particular facts. These sound natural and right.[40]

Another thing we need to grasp in order to understand Lewis' analysis of counterfactual asymmetry is his notion of an asymmetric over-determination structure of the world.[41] To understand this structure, first notice that a *determinant* is understood to be 'a minimal set of conditions jointly sufficient, given the laws of nature, for

---

[40] There is some noticeable vagueness in these criteria of similarity. But Lewis thinks, which we can agree, that the vagueness is rather a merit of his theory. After all, our intuition about counterfactuals is rarely clear-cut.

[41] According to Lewis, that there is such a structure in the world is only an empirical claim.

the fact in question.' [1979: 474] For simplicity, let's only consider the 'set of conditions' and the 'fact' to be particular occurrences of events. As far as particular occurrences of events are concerned, we can say that event A is a determinant of event B if and only if, provided certain laws of nature, the occurrence of A is minimally sufficient for the occurrence of B.[42] Now, according to Lewis, the asymmetric over-determination structure that is crucial to his analysis of counterfactual asymmetry consists in an empirical fact that, in the actual world, *an event always has many more later determinants than earlier determinants*. This structure is what he calls *'the asymmetry of over-determination'*.

(A few passing comments: It is easy to see that the over-determination by earlier determinants is just what I called at the beginning of this chapter 'the causal over-determination', in which each individual cause-event is by itself sufficient for the effect-event, such as in the example in which two gunmen simultaneously shot the

---

[42] For simplicity in what follows when I need to refer to the occurrence of an event, or the fact that the event occurs, I only elliptically say the name of the event, unless when this sounds confusing.

victim to death. Admittedly, cases like this are very rare. What worries me, however, is that the so-called overdetermination by *later determinants* is a structure of what I have called 'the common-cause fork'. In defining this fork I didn't say that every joint effect in the fork is sufficient for the common cause. I still think, pace Lewis, that to regard the joint effects in a common-cause fork as *individually* sufficient for the common cause is problematic.[43] Perhaps what Lewis has in mind is only an *inferential* relation—that is, from each and every joint effect it can be inferred that there must have been the common cause. But this claim is not trivial. In exactly what sense can we infer from a single joint effect that there must have been the common cause? Lewis didn't explain. At any rate, the explanation cannot be that the world is strictly and totally deterministic (this is an assumption Lewis does appear to hold in his discussion). If it is because of radical determinism that a joint effect is said to be sufficient for the common cause, then for the same reason it can also be said that, in a common-effect fork, each and every joint cause is sufficient for the

---

[43] As we discussed in Ch. 1, it is even not clear in what sense *any* effect can be regarded as a sufficient condition for its causes.

common effect as well. Obviously, Lewis would never want to say this. Otherwise he would commit himself in saying that an event's earlier determinants are as usual as, and as many as, its later determinants, and thus the notion of the asymmetry of over-determination would lose its whole point. But, let's not be detained by this problem. My criticism of Lewis' analysis of counterfactual asymmetry is not meant to be an external one. Let's grant that Lewis is right about the asymmetry of over-determination and see what follows.)

So much for the background. Equipped with the tools introduced earlier, Lewis' analysis of counterfactual asymmetry can be explained by making use of some diagrams. First, let's see why a normal, *forward-tracking*, counterfactual—'If C had not occurred, then E would not have occurred'—is true. Suppose that in our actual world, $w0$, C and E occur and are lawfully connected. Suppose also that there are two possible worlds, $w1$ and $w2$. In $w1$, neither C nor E occurs, whereas in $w2$, C does not occur but E does. Which of the two possible worlds, then, is more similar to the actual world? Consider Figure 6. (Note that in all the following figures the lines stand for laws of nature, the arrows indicate temporal, *not causal*, asymmetries between lawfully connected events.

Causal Asymmetry and Causal Forks

According to Lewis, causal dependence stems from counterfactual dependence; in following him to analyze counterfactual asymmetry we should not make use of the notion of causal asymmetry, otherwise the analysis would be circular.)

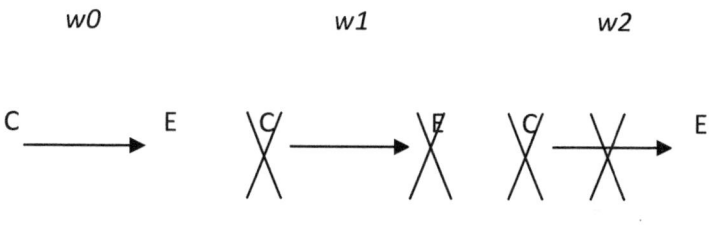

Figure 6

In *w2*, given the non-occurrence of C (indicated by putting a cross on C), the occurrence of E can only obtain at the expense of a violation of the law (indicated by putting a cross on the line, which stands for the law) in virtue of which C and E are connected.[44] Clearly, *w1*, in which two particular facts—i.e., the occurrence of C and that of E—are absent, is more similar to the actual world than *w2*, in which one particular fact—i.e., the occurrence of C—is absent, *and a law is violated as well*. So the counterfactual 'If C had not occurred, then E would not have occurred' is true, in that *w1*, in which both the antecedent and the consequent are true—i.e., both C and E do not occur—is more similar to the actual world than *w2*, in which the antecedent is true but the consequent is false—i.e., C does not occur but E does.

But now the back-tracking argument kicks in. It may be pointed out that *w1*, which is more similar to the actual world than *w2*, is also more similar to the actual world than another possible world, *w3*, in which E does not occur but C does.

---

[44] I take it that, given determinism, a law is violated if and only if either, *but not both*, of two events C and E, which are connected in virtue of the law, does not occur. When both C and E do not occur, the law is merely uninstantiated, not violated.

Causal Asymmetry and Causal Forks

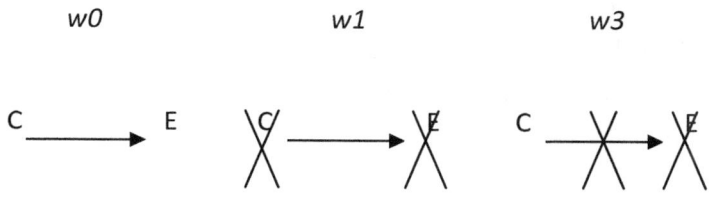

Figure 7

It appears so, as long as we want to keep in line with the reasoning just given in support of the forward-tracking counterfactual. According to the same reasoning, we should say that the counterfactual 'If E had not occurred, then C would not have occurred' is true, since *w1*, in which only two particular facts are absent is more similar to the actual world than *w3*, in which a particular fact is absent, and a law is violated as well.

According to Lewis, however, what really happens in the case of the back-tracking counterfactual is not as simple as Figure 7 suggests. Suppose that in the actual world, *w0*, C has three *later determinants*: E, F, and G.[45] Now, let's consider two possible worlds, in one of which, *w1*, both C and E do not occur and in the other of which, *w3*, E does not occur but C does. Then we have:

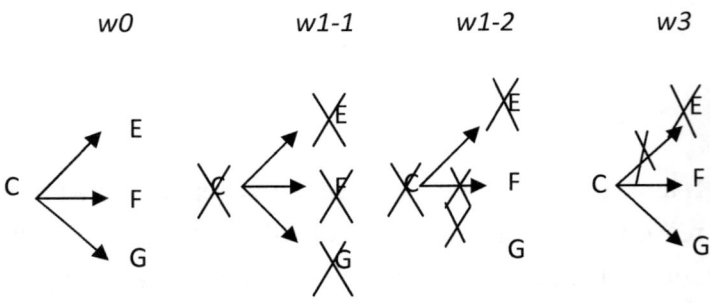

Figure 8

---

[45] Lewis contends that earlier determinants of C are few and unusual, and need not be considered in comparing possible worlds. But this contention may be challenged, as we will see shortly in Price's criticism of Lewis.

Note that there can be at least two varieties of *w1*. In *w1-1*, F and G do not occur, but the laws, in virtue of which C is connected respectively with F and G are retained; in *w1-2*, F and G both occur, but the laws are violated. No doubt, there can still be other varieties of *w1*, for example a world *w1-3*, in which everything is like *w1-1* except the fact that G occurs and the law in virtue of which C and G are connected is violated, and so on. But the important point is that, in any variety of *w1*, C does not occur, and to accommodate the non-occurrence of C in such a world some significant adjustments of laws and/or other particular facts need to be made. This is because there are many determinants of C, for example F and G, which are in virtue of certain laws sufficient for C. And thus in any *coherent* stipulation of *w1*, to stipulate the non-occurrence of C either means to stipulate the non-occurrence of those determinants of C, or to stipulate the violation of certain laws in virtue of which these determinants are sufficient for C. *w3*, by contrast, is a world in which C occurs. To stipulate such a world, there is no need to make any adjustment with respect to C's determinants such as F and G, or the laws in virtue of which they are sufficient for C.

Now, it is easy to see that *w3* is more similar to the actual world than *w1-2*, since there are more particular facts absent as well as more laws violated in *w1-2*. What about *w3* as opposed to *w1-1*? Recall that one of the criteria in comparing possible worlds' similarities to the actual world is that some minor violation of law weighs less than a massive absence of particular facts. In *w3*, the law in virtue of which the C and E are connected is violated, but three particular facts, C, F, and G, are not absent. Note that the example as we describe it is for illustration. In reality it is very likely that there are many more determinants of C than we named here. In view of this, a world, in which a great many particular facts—i.e. those determinants of C—obtain, must be more similar to the actual world than another world, in which a single law obtains only at the expense of these many facts. Hence, it seems reasonable to say that *w3* is more similar to the actual world than *w1-1*. And if *w3* is more similar to the actual world than both *w1-1* and *w1-2*, and presumably any other variety of *w1*, then we can conclude that *w3*, in which E does not occur but C does, is more similar to the actual world than any *w1*, in which both E and C do not occur. From this it follows that, according to Lewis' semantics of counterfactuals, the counterfactual, 'If E had not occurred, then C would not have occurred', is false, as desired.[46]

In criticizing Lewis' analysis, I shall first evaluate a not quite successful criticism made by Price [1992][47], the

---

[46] Some may worry that the introduction of determinants of C may in some way affect Lewis' initial argument in showing the forward-tracking counterfactual, namely 'If C had not occurred, then E would not have occurred', to be true. It will not. Look again at Figure 6. In the forward-tracking counterfactual, the stipulation we begin with is not the non-occurrence of E, but that of C. It is not hard to see that no matter how many determinants of C are introduced into w_1, they can be introduced into w_2 as well. Given the non-occurrence of C, we can either retain a determinant of C by allowing a violation of the law in virtue of which C and the determinant is connected, or else retain the law by allowing the non-occurrence of the determinant. Either way, what is stipulated in w_1 can all the same be stipulated in w_2. No difference between the two possible worlds can be derived from a consideration of the over-determination of C. Lewis' argument about the forward-tracking counterfactual thus stands irrespective of this complication involving the over-determination structure of the world.

[47] Henceforth all references made to Hausman are from this work.

discussion of which will pave the way to understanding my own objection to Lewis' analysis.

Price's criticism of Lewis' analysis of counterfactual asymmetry and for that matter his analysis of causal asymmetry consists in saying that, given a time-symmetric nature of physical theory, Lewis' analysis is unsatisfactory in accounting for causal asymmetry in microphysics. More exactly, the objection is:

> This [Lewis'] approach cannot make sense of our causal intuitions with respect to microphysics, or more generally what we might call 'the physics of the very few'. Here the fork asymmetry is absent because it depends on the statistical behaviour of large numbers of physical entities. The attempt to ground causal asymmetry on the fork asymmetry thus turns out to conflict with the reductionist intuition that macrocausation consists of a lot of little bits of microcausation, as well as with the fact that physicists are inclined to speak of asymmetric causation even in microphysics. [502]

First, a small point about this objection. It is true that Lewis grounds causal asymmetry on counterfactual asymmetry, and in turn grounds counterfactual asymmetry on a kind of fork asymmetry (i.e., what he calls 'the asymmetry of over-determination', or what I identified as a difference between the causal over-determination and the common-cause fork). But I am not sure to what extent the fork structure Lewis has in mind bears on the so-called 'statistical behaviour of large numbers of physical entities' as Price accuses. It appears that, to appreciate Lewis' analysis, we need not consult any statistical feature of the fork structure. Actually, as Price mentioned in a note [503], Lewis himself complained about Price's characterizing his view as associated with statistics.

But under a certain interpretation Price's objection still has some force. The gist of his objection, to recapitulate, is that on the micro-level the so-called asymmetry of over-determination disappears; a microscopic event normally has as many—more precisely, as *few*—earlier determinants as later determinants. So the conception of this symmetry is based on a biased observation made on the macro-level. Maybe the macro-level asymmetry is essentially statistical, or maybe it is not. But this does not really matter that much for Price's criticism. As long as he can show that there is no such a thing as the asymmetry of over-determination on the *micro-level*, and vindicate the quite appealing *reductionist intuition* that macro-level relations (including, of course, causal asymmetry) only obtain in virtue of the micro-level relations, he will then inflict a considerable blow on Lewis' analysis.

Why is there no asymmetry of over-determination on the micro-level? Price makes his point by developing the famous Nixon case, a well-known case designed as an objection to Lewis' semantics of counterfactuals which aims to show that Lewis' semantics will unduly render the following sentence false:

(1) If Nixon had pressed the button, there would have been a nuclear war.

Lewis' semantics of counterfactuals is false, for, it is argued, a possible world in which Nixon presses the button but the nuclear disaster somehow does not follow is clearly more similar to the actual world than another possible world in which Nixon presses the button and the disaster follows. Remember that, in comparing possible worlds with respect to their similarity to the actual world, the perfect match of a great many particular facts may weigh more than the perfect match of a single law of nature. (At any rate, between saving the world from the nuclear disaster and saving a single law the choice is not hard to make.) So, it seems that, in order to accommodate Nixon's pressing of the button in a possible world and make the world overall more similar to the actual world, we better allow a unlawful 'miracle'—for instance, a mysterious breakdown of the signal sent out by Nixon's pressing the button—to avoid the nuclear missiles' launch and thus the disaster, rather than allow the disaster to lawfully follow. So, according to Lewis' semantics of counterfactuals, (1) is false. But, intuitively, it is not.

Lewis' reply [1979: 469-70] to this objection is based on his observation that there are many more effects—or, as it were, traces—of Nixon's pressing the button than we usually realize. His fingerprints are left on the button; he is shaken by what he did; his gin bottle is depleted; the click of the button has been preserved on tape; light waves that carry the image of his finger on the button flow out the window; so on and so forth. Besides, small differences give rise to bigger differences sooner or later, and it is likely that these inconspicuous effects will end up generating something big. As a result, the apparent alikeness between the actual world and the world in which the button is pressed but the nuclear disaster is stopped by a small miracle cannot really last very long. They will diverge considerably from each other sooner or later, and eventually become totally different worlds—this is so, especially when we consider that determinism is true in both of the two worlds, such that little differences will almost for sure lead to big ones.

Sure enough, it may be suggested that widespread and complicated miracles can be set up not only to prevent the nuclear disaster but also wipe up all the traces of Nixon's pressing of the button. But, obviously in this case there are just too many laws of nature violated, and a world like this must be very much unlike the actual world as we know it. [Lewis 1979: 470-1]

Now, the situation appears to be this. As far as a possible world in which Nixon presses the nuclear button and the nuclear disaster is stopped by a small miracle is concerned, either we can coherently stipulate (i) that in such a world the traces of the pressing of the button will develop such that the world will eventually end up being totally different from the actual world anyway; or (ii) that in such a world those traces of the pressing of the button will, just like what happens to the nuclear disaster, also be stopped by even more miracles. It is unlikely, however, that the possible world stipulated either way is more similar to the actual world than another possible world in which Nixon presses the button, no miracle happens, and then the world just continues in its lawful course—that is, the nuclear disaster just unfolds.

Are the pictures depicted in Lewis' reply plausible? No, says Price, if we focus on what happens in the *micro-level* worlds, rather than that in the *macro-level* ones. Suppose that we replace the macroscopic event of Nixon's pressing the button with some appropriate microscopic event, say, the disappearance of marble Ω in Nixon's brain. This is to say, if Nixon loses this marble at the crucial moment of his decision-making (time T) then given the circumstances and the laws of nature he will definitely press the button. Given these reasonable assumptions, the following counterfactual seems to be true:

(2) If marble Ω had ceased to exist at T, there would have been a nuclear war.

Price then argues:

> The difficulty for Lewis is that in virtue of the microscopic nature of the counterfactual event in question, it is not overdetermined by its effects, in the manner required to generate an asymmetry for miracles. The miracle required to restore the actual course of history, in the event that Ω does cease to exist at T, is not diverse and widespread. It is simply that Ω should come into existence again between T and t2 [a time when Ω is supposed to collide with some other marble], with whatever position and momentum it would have had if had not ceased to exist in the first place. There are no records or traces to adjust in the world. [507]

The idea is that usually a microscopic event does not have multiple effects; or, in Lewis' terminology, the idea is that a microscopic event is *not* over-determined by later determinants. So in order to make as much agreement as possible between a possible world in which Nixon loses marble Ω with the actual world in which he does not, not many miracles in the possible world need to be stipulated. As far as the possible world *on the micro-level* is concerned, to bring things back on track what we need to do is just to stipulate, as a small miracle, marble Ω comes into existence shortly after its disappearance. In order to accommodate the disappearance of the marble in the possible world, few changes other than the single miracle need to be made. Therefore, from the point of view of the micro-level, Lewis' claim (ii)—i.e., in a possible world in order to accommodate Nixon's pressing of the nuclear button a lot of miracles need to be stipulated so as to bring the world back on track (i.e., the actual track of the actual world)—is simply wrong. If we set our sights on the microphysical world, Lewis' proposed asymmetry of over-determination does not really exist and, as a result, his account of causal asymmetry hinging upon this asymmetry of over-determination, collapses. Since we are inclined to think, inspired by the reductionist intuition, that causal asymmetry exhibited in the macrophysical world must have a certain corresponding asymmetry as its basis in the microphysical world. If causal asymmetry in the microphysical world cannot be accounted for by appeal to the asymmetry of over-determination, it is unlikely that it can be in the macrophysical world.

There are still some other details of Price's criticism, but its major point has been presented. This criticism, however, is not decisive, in at least the following two aspects. First, as Lewis points out in correspondence [Price: 508], 'the world of [the marble Ω] example differs from the world we take to be ours in more ways than meet the eye: it's not just a world of classical physics! Do marbles act as gravitational sources? Do they interact with the electromagnetic field? If so, then after a marble miraculously disappears, you won't get reconvergence just by putting the marble back (with appropriate position and velocity).' At this point I am sympathetic to Lewis' position. Even if Lewis supposes too many determinants for a macroscopic event, it appears that Price just supposes too few for a microscopic one.

More importantly, perhaps the reductionism that is needed in Price's criticism is wrong; perhaps it is not the case that causal asymmetry on the macro-level can be adequately reduced to that on the micro-level. At any rate, it is not unusual to suggest that there are at least some macro-level features that are irreducible to micro-level ones. Why cannot causal asymmetry be just one of them?

Of course, a non-reductionist need not deny that in a certain sense there is causal asymmetry on the micro-level too. She may say that the micro-level causal asymmetry is derivative, and is in some way projected from the notion of the macro-level causal asymmetry proper. It is true that the non-reductionist then faces the problem of making sense of this projection. But the reductionist on the other hand faces the problem of making sense of reduction. There seem to be no obvious advantage on the reductionist's part.

Now, while Price's criticism consists in saying in effect that Lewis makes too much out of the over-determination, I suggest the opposite. By this I do not mean that Lewis posits too few *immediate* determinants for a given event—he posits quite a few and quite enough. The problem, however, is that he fails to consider that those determinants he posits have their own even further determinants. Moving one step further, we will see that Lewis' argument, which only takes a one-step over-determination relation into consideration, does not really work.

The above idea can be better explained by making use of some of diagrams again. Have a look again at Figure 6. To recapitulate, the argument in support of the truthfulness of the forward-tracking counterfactual, 'If C had not occurred, then E would not have occurred', is roughly this. Both *w1* and *w2* are stipulated to be such a way as to accommodate the non-occurrence of C. But *w1*, in which only two particular facts are sacrificed, is more similar to the actual world than *w2*, in which one particular fact as well as a law is sacrificed. The counterfactual, 'If C had not occurred, then E would not have occurred', is therefore true, since the world in which both the antecedent and the consequent are true—i.e., *w1*—is more similar to the actual world than the possible world in which the antecedent is true but the consequent is false—i.e., *w2*.

The point I am here concerned with is, however, that E has its own later determinants. In line with Lewis' thought on over-determination, it is natural to suppose that E has many later determinants, for instance F1, F2, and F3. Instead of Figure 6, the following diagram is more likely to be the case:

Causal Asymmetry and Causal Forks

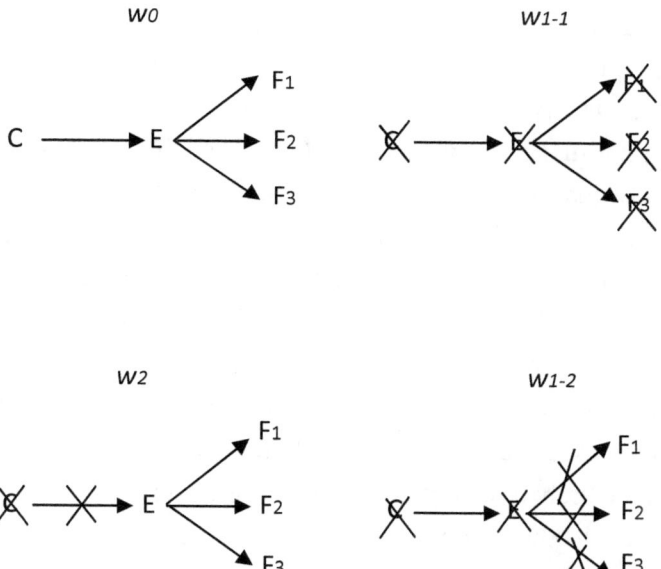

Figure 9

In a possible world in which E is to be removed in a coherent way, the non-occurrence of E requires that certain adjustments be made to its later determinants, or to the laws in virtue of which E and its later determinants are connected. *w1* is such a kind of world. Note that again there are two typical varieties of *w1*. In coherently stipulating E to be absent in *w1*, we can stipulate E's later determinants also to be absent (this is *w1-1*); or, we can stipulate that the laws in virtue of which E and these determinants are connected are violated (this is *w1-2*). Obviously, *w1-2*, in which two particular facts are absent and three laws violated, is less similar to the actual world than *w2*, in which only one particular fact is absent and one law violated. Less obviously but still very likely, *w1-1*, in which five particular facts are absent, is also less similar to the actual world than *w2*. (Presumably E has many more later determinants than named here—remember that the perfect match of a great many particular facts may well outweigh the perfect match of a single law.) There are still other varieties of *w1*, depending on how the absences of the particular facts and the violations of the laws are combined. But it seems that no matter whether we stipulate that *w1* features great loss of particular facts (the occurrences of the later determinants of E), great loss of laws (the laws in virtue of which E and its later determinants are connected), or a combination of both to a lesser degree, it is unlikely that *w1* can be less of a departure from actuality than *w2*, in which only one particular fact (i.e., the occurrence of C) is absent and one law (the law in virtue of which C and E are connected) violated. It is therefore unlikely that there is any variety of *w1* in which both C and E do not occur is more similar to the actual world than *w2* in which C does not occur but E does. If so, then, according to Lewis' semantics of counterfactuals, the forward-tracking counterfactual 'If C had not occurred, then E would not have occurred' is likely to be false. His argument for endorsing the forward-tracking counterfactual is thus problematic.

Note, however, that Lewis' argument to falsify the *back-tracking* counterfactual 'If E had not occurred, then C would not have occurred' is not problematic, not at least for the same reason as to why his argument to endorse the *forward-tracking* counterfactual is problematic. Have a look at Figure 7. It is not difficult to see that whether or not we take into consideration of the later determinants of E does not really matter for Lewis' argument for the falsity of the back-tracking counterfactual. In both *w1* and *w3*, E is stipulated to be absent. No matter how other parts of *w1* need to be adjusted in order to accommodate the absence of E, the same adjustment need to be made in *w3* too. So it seems that Lewis' argument to falsify the back-tracking counterfactual stands anyway.

But our earlier argument that Lewis is unsuccessful in endorsing the forward-tracking counterfactual is enough to show that Lewis' analysis of counterfactual asymmetry resting on the asymmetry of overdetermination is implausible. Obviously, in order for the counterfactual asymmetry to hold, both the back-tracking counterfactual needs to be falsified, and the forward-tracking counterfactual needs to be justified. Intuitively, it may still be felt that the forward-tracking counterfactual is right but the back-tracking one is somehow wrong, but it seems that this intuition needs to be explained by some other means rather than the analysis Lewis has offered.

It is easy to see that these conclusions we reach may have an important impact on the counterfactual theory of causation, so far as Lewis' version of that theory is concerned. But this interesting question cannot be pursued here. For my limited purpose, it suffices to say that, since Lewis' analysis of counterfactual asymmetry is itself problematic, it cannot render reliable support to Ehring's analysis of causal asymmetry. Alternatively put, the idea is that Lewis' analysis can show, as needed by Ehring's analysis, that in a common-cause fork the common cause is not counterfactually dependent on any of the joint effects, but only at the expense of undermining normal forward-tracking counterfactuals. Ehring would of course never want to give up forward-tracking counterfactuals, otherwise he would not be able to make sense of the notion of a (genuine) condition that is crucial to his analysis of causal asymmetry. Can Ehring, then, just buy Lewis' analysis of back-tracking counterfactuals but neglect the analysis of forward-tracking ones? Apparently not. Lewis' analysis of counterfactuals—both forward-tracking and back-tracking—is derived from a general semantics as well as an understanding of a general over-determination structure of the world. So you cannot just buy his analysis of back-tracking counterfactuals, without worrying that the defect of his analysis of forward-tracking counterfactuals is rooted in some defect of his general doctrines, which actually in turn makes the plausibility of his analysis of back-tracking counterfactuals only superficial.

To summarize this chapter, I think that enough justice has been done to the idea that causal asymmetry is analyzable in terms of fork structures. Hausman's analysis does not work, since his crucial definition of a causal connection is ad hoc; Ehring's analysis does not improve upon Hausman's, since his crucial definition of a condition, under close scrutiny, does not discriminate in the required way; and, finally, Lewis' analysis of counterfactual asymmetry does not assist Ehring's account, since the analysis itself is problematic. It therefore seems to me safe to say that causal asymmetry cannot be adequately accounted for by appeal to fork structures.

Chapter 3

Borderline Cases (I): Simultaneous Causation and Backwards Causation

3.1 Introduction

3.2 Simultaneous Causation

3.3 Backwards Causation

3.1 Introduction

The conclusions drawn from the discussion in the previous two chapters are largely negative. Both of the two major theories of causation, the regularity theory and the counterfactual theory, turn out to be inadequate when it comes to accounting for causal asymmetry. Perhaps there is a chance, however slim, that these theories can be modified or re-interpreted in some way that we may have failed to consider so as to do the job better. Nevertheless, there is a danger that to significantly modify or re-interpret of a general theory of causation merely for the purpose of accounting for causal asymmetry might have to sacrifice some other merits of the theory. Although causal asymmetry is thought to be one of the essential features of causation, those major theories of causation are not primarily designed for the purpose of accounting for this feature. Adjusting them in a way that suits this particular purpose better, while retaining their merits in all the other important respects, seems to be a work that, if possible at all, is too extensive to be undertaken here.

I suggest that we try something different. In this chapter and the next, my strategy is to examine several *borderline cases* of causation, cases in which whether a certain causal relation (and thus the causal asymmetry involved) can be said to hold or not becomes problematic—that is, both sides of the issue can be argued, but neither conclusively. Presumably, our intuition about causal asymmetry will become sharper by considering these cases; and we will thus be in an advantageous position to see what the notion of causal asymmetry really consists in. No doubt, strategies of this kind are not

Borderline Cases (I)

unusual in dealing with various other issues, particularly in working out a definition. Suppose that we want to define what a table is. One way to proceed is to draw attention to cases where there are good reasons to think that an object is a table but there are also good reasons to think that it is not. Considerations of this kind are heuristically advisable, for the obvious reason that, by checking along the borderline cases of tables, we can narrow down the nature of a table. In a similar manner, it can be hoped that a study of borderline cases of causation will help narrow down the nature of causal asymmetry.

There are three borderline cases I want to discuss in this chapter: simultaneous causation, backwards causation, and causation involving absences as causal relata. Obviously, something in general can be said about simultaneous causation and backwards causation. In the majority of cases of causation, causes, as a matter of fact, precede their effects. But whether causes *always*, or even *must*, precede their effects can be in doubt. Having acknowledged that an event does not precede another, what the advocates of simultaneous causation and of backwards causation both aim to do, therefore, is either to vindicate, as a strong claim, that the first event nevertheless causes the other, or, as a weak claim, that it *could* cause the other. By contrast, an adherent of the sequential theory of causation[48], according to whom causes always, or even *must*, precede their effects, will try to argue that those putative cases of the so-called simultaneous causation or backwards causation are either not genuine causal relations, or, despite their appearance at first glance, under closer scrutiny will turn out to be merely sequential causal relations nevertheless. Even though I am not convinced by the sequentialist's argument, taking sides is not the point here. What is important, as we will see, is to bring to light a controversy that underlies the surface disagreement between the two sides. It is this underlying controversy, rather than the two sides themselves, that will point in the direction of how to properly understand causal asymmetry.

---

[48] This term is borrowed from Huemer and Kovitz [2003: 556]

Borderline Cases (I)

3.2 Simultaneous Causation

A simultaneous causal relation is supposed to be a causal relation such that the cause event and its effect event[49] occur at the same time, or, in the case where the cause and the effect last a certain period of time, during the same period of time. Since the most obvious way to prove that something of a certain kind is possible is to present just such a thing, the advocate of simultaneous causation often argues by suggesting examples that are, prima facie, cases of simultaneous causation. Let's follow this practice in our discussion, and check one by one how those suggested examples may be evaluated.

To begin with, it may be said that there are cases of *instantaneous transmission of force*, in which, roughly speaking, the causal process in question is supposed to complete instantaneously, so that there is no temporal interval whatsoever between the cause and the effect. To give an idea, here are two examples from the literature:

---

[49] For simplicity I will only talk about events—broadly construed as including statistic states—as causal relata.

(1) A locomotive pulls a caboose to move [Taylor 1973: 35];

(2) Moving one end of a pencil causes the other end to move [Tooley 1987: 207].

These cases may be challenged, however, either by referring to the notion of rigidity of physical bodies, or to the Special Theory of Relativity (STR). Roughly, the rigidity postulation says that both the body of the train and that of the pencil, actually any physical body in reality, are not perfectly rigid. The crucial thing here is to notice that, in (1) for example, before the caboose is pulled to move, there has to be, under the pulling force applied by the locomotive, some slight deformation of the connecting part between the locomotive and the caboose[50], so that a resisting force in the connecting part is generated to balance the pulling force. It is this resisting force, rather than the pulling force from the locomotive as

---

[50] Strictly speaking, there was a chain of successive deformations all along the body of the train, from the engine of the locomotive till the wheels of the caboose. To see the point, though, there is no need to get into the details.

such, that directly applies to the caboose and makes it move, or continue to move (against resistance of the track, air, etc). Since any deformation, or generation of resisting force, takes time, the so-called 'pull' cannot be instantaneous; and therefore the movement of the locomotive and that of the caboose cannot be simultaneous. Likewise, similar things can be said about (2).

In addition, a more straightforward way to look at the issue is to think about STR. According to STR, no physical influence can be transmitted at unlimited speed. Consequently, there must be certain temporal intervals for physical influences to be transmitted between spatially separated causes and effects. In (2), it simply cannot be the case that the momentum from one end of the pencil is transmitted instantaneously to the other end to make it move. Strictly speaking, there is no such thing as the both ends' moving together at the same time. Likewise, similar considerations apply to (1).

Now, besides cases of instantaneous transmission of force, it may be said that there are cases of *contact*, in which it appears that the ideas of rigidity or STR are not directly applicable. Consider Kant's well-known example [*Critique*: A203]:

(3) A lead ball is sitting on a cushion, causing
a hollow shape formed in the latter.

In dealing with examples like this, a little more elaboration is needed. To start with, it can be pointed out that, to identify the sitting of the ball as the cause is an ordinary but vague way of describing the case. More precisely and in the language of physics, we better say that the formation of the hollow is caused by the *momentum* of the ball. The matter being put this way, it seems legitimate then to ask where the momentum of the ball lies *exactly*. However, as Kline [1980: 299] argues at this point, if the momentum of the ball is located at its centre of mass, or however slightly distant from its surface, then, as we have seen in those alleged cases of instantaneous transmission of force, some time is still needed to transfer the momentum. On the other hand, if it is maintained that the momentum of the ball is located on its surface (the part of its surface that is in touch with the cushion) and there is no separation whatsoever between the surface of the ball and the surface of the cushion, then it seems that the momentum of the ball will just become *identical* to the momentum of the formation of the hollow. To put it another way, according to this latter understanding of the ball's momentum, the original putative cause (the sitting of the ball) and its putative effect (the formation of the hollow) become just two different *descriptions* of one and the same event. Suppose we agree that no event can be self-caused, it follows that there is no real causal relation going on in the cushion example.

I have so far briefly presented the matter in a way that is quite unfavourable to the advocate of simultaneous causation—she argues by suggesting examples, but as we have seen those examples she suggests are either shown to be dubious cases of simultaneity, or to be dubious cases of causation at all, let alone simultaneous causation. Facing a situation like this, it seems better for her to retreat from the strong claim that there are *actual* cases of simultaneous causation, and turn to argue the weak claim that there *could* be such cases. In other words, it may be argued that, even though as a matter of fact there are no cases of simultaneous causation, the notion of simultaneous causation, given certain ideal conditions, can nevertheless be made intelligible.

Before unfolding this idea, however, let's step back for a moment and try to view the whole matter of simultaneous causation from a broader perspective. While causation is a long-standing topic in metaphysics, the notion of *simultaneity* largely belongs to the domain of empirical science. Being familiar with the idea of modern science and technology, one can come up with a definition of simultaneity that is as precisely as one wants.[51] Against some more precise standard, a previously settled notion of simultaneity can be easily, and, according to scientific measures, uncontroversially, rejected. In a case-by-case debate, the advocate of the notion of simultaneous causation, the metaphysician, will inevitably find herself in a disadvantageous position: whenever she suggests a case of simultaneous causation, her opponent, the scientist, can simply point out that, according to some more precise measurement, it is not a real case of simultaneity after all! Thus understood, the surface difficulty of the notion of simultaneous causation is only an empirical one—as a matter of fact, an irrefutable case of simultaneity is hard to obtain. But, simply because of this empirical difficulty, it does not follow that simultaneous causation is *conceptually* impossible.

---

[51] A modern atomic clock can easily achieve an accuracy of 10^{-9} second per day.

Borderline Cases (I)

Let's, then, shift to *ideal* cases. If there were an ideal, though maybe never empirically attainable, case of simultaneity, what would it be like? Here is a simple example. Suppose that a switch is connected to two identically made bulbs, via two pieces of equal-length and identically made wire. Actually, for peace of mind, I suggest that we can just suppose that the two bulbs are duplicates of each other, as well as the two pieces of wire. Now, the device with this setting works in a simple way: whenever I turn on the switch, two electronic signals are sent to the two bulbs respectively and then they will light.

In the posited scenario, it appears safe to say that the two bulbs light simultaneously: given the fact that the two electronic signals are sent at the same time by one and the same switching, travel two equal distances through two duplicate pieces of wire, and then trigger two duplicate bulbs to light, it seems gratuitous to suggest otherwise.[52] Of course, so far in this scenaio there is no simultaneous causation yet; it is only that the two bulbs' lightings are

---

[52] To rule out complications of STR, let's suppose that there is no relative movement between any two objects we mentioned in the example, and that the observer in the example's setting, who is at a same distance away from the two bulbs, is also relatively still to all those objects.

caused by my *prior* turning on of the switch. Suppose, however, that both of the two bulbs are made in such a way that they, when *individually* connected to the switch and triggered, will *randomly* light red, green or blue. So for example when individually connected to the switch and first turned on, one of the bulbs, bulb A, lights red; the second time, blue; etc. The point is, after many experiments, no regularity whatsoever in bulb A's individual lighting sequence is recognizable. In a similar way, bulb B's individual lighting sequence is also observed as random.

Interesting things happen, however, once I connect both of the random-lighting bulbs to the switch: whenever I turn on the switch, both of them light the *same* colour. Every time, they *both* light either red, green or blue. So even though the lighting sequence for each of them, individually speaking, is still random, their lighting sequences now become strictly coordinated to each other. Now, given the fact that after hundreds of experiments, the two bulbs, when both connected to the switch, always light the same colour upon my switching, should I infer that there is some kind of simultaneous causation between their lighting up the same colour, or should I insist that their harmonious lighting up is just a matter of chance?

It should be noted in passing that the question I have in mind is not whether the two bulbs, despite their superficial random lightings, have some underlying deterministic mechanism such that their lightings are coordinated in a way unbeknown to us. Also, I will not consider the possibility that the perfect match between the two bulbs' lighting sequences is, to use Leibniz's term, a "pre-established harmony". In short, I take it that the two bulbs' individual lighting sequences are *tout court* random. True, it may be said that, since the two bulbs are made exactly like each other, it is only to be expected that they have the same lighting sequence—no matter *how* exactly the sequence obtains. But I am not supposing, as it would be unusual, that the two bulbs are always turned on together during their whole lives. Suppose that, on every occasion that they are turned on together, bulb A, individually speaking, is being turned on for the ith time, whereas the bulb B is being turned on for its $(i+1)$th time. On this supposition, given the fact that the two bulbs are duplicates of each other and the fact that they both light randomly (even if the lightings' being random are based on a same mechanism!), different lightings should be expected indeed.

Facing with the results we got in the experiments, we can choose to say either of two things: i) A's lighting up a colour and B's lighting up the same colour are simultaneously causally related, or else ii) the same lightings are merely by chance. Note that, by stipulation, this is an ideal case of simultaneous lightings. So if there is any problem as to whether there is a simultaneous *causal* relation between these lightings, the problem is with causation, not simultaneity. I admit that it is difficult to tell whether the same lightings are causally related. We want to say yes to this question, because otherwise the correlation between the two lightings is hard to make sense. But we also want to say no, because there seems to be no recognizable physical *mediator* between the two lightings[53], and causation as we usually understand it does

---

[53] The two bulbs, of course, are mediated via their connections to the switch. But these two connections cannot help explain why the two bulbs light with the *same* colour, but only why they light at all (obviously, the explanation is a usual one, namely that the cause is my prior switching). It should be noted, however, that the thought experiment I give here is inspired by Bell's phenomenon. According to one explanation of this phenomenon there can be, via the connections to the switch, backwards causation from one bulb's lighting up a

not work that way. Usually, we take it that if two physical occurrences are to be causally connected, they have to be *physically* connected in the first place. Thus, to adopt the first answer, we have to allow the spooky 'action at a distance', whereas to adopt the second, we have to allow inexplicable coincidences, happening at a frequency that seems no less spooky.

Fortunately, for our limited purpose we don't have to decide on this hard question. Our aim is to track down the nature of causal asymmetry, not that of causation as such. So, for the sake of argument, simply assume that there is a causal relation between A's lighting a certain colour and B's lighting that colour too, and focus on the question as to how to make sense of which causes which.

But even in connection with this less ambitious question it appears that we don't have much to say. Actually, an important reason why in this thought experiment it is hard to tell for sure whether there is a

---

certain colour to the other's also lighting up that colour. In other words, what happens is that one bulb receives a signal to light a certain colour first, and then somehow sends feedback to the switch such that the switch *sent* out the signal that *triggered* the other bulb to light that colour too. I neglect this complication. For a discussion, see Price [1994].

causal relation between A's lighting up a certain colour and B's lighting up that colour too is that there appears to be no way for us to tell, between the two, which one is in *any* sense prior, let alone causally prior. In the majority cases of sequential causation, we can judge the cause-effect distinction by checking two events' temporal order. Even though, as I emphasized several times before, the causal order is neither equivalent nor reducible to the temporal order, as a rule of thumb in practice it is often useful to pin down the former in the light of the latter. But, in a case of simultaneous occurrence of two events, the lack of temporal order will render the causal order especially obscure.

What, then, do we need, in deciding whether A's lighting up a certain colour causes B's lighting up that colour or whether it is the other way around? In trying to answer this question, we now come to the core of the problem of causal asymmetry. Suppose that, as a modification to the original example, B always lights *regularly*, or at any rate in a deterministic way. Its lighting sequence has been found to be, say, first red, then blue, then green, and then the pattern repeats over and over again. A, on the other hand, when individually connected to the switch, still lights randomly. But, as we supposed before, when both connected to the switch, the two bulbs' lightings are somehow synchronized—A begins to light regularly as well, in the same sequence as that of B, i.e., first red, then blue, then green, and so on.

Facing this scenario, I contend that the intuitively correct thing to say is that B's lighting a certain colour causes A to light that colour, rather than the other way around (given, of course, we first agree that they are causally connected). The reason to back this intuition, as I see it, is that B's lighting sequence is *explanatorily prior* to that of A's. About the notion of explanatory priority I will say more in Ch. 6. It suffices to say at this stage that, when the two bulbs are both connected to the switch and A begins to light regularly, that A lights this way is a piece of newly obtained information, which is then in need of explanation. On the other hand, it makes little sense to say that, when both connected, the fact that A lights regularly explains why B also lights regularly—B *always* lights regularly, and its explanation, if any, should be independent of the newly obtained fact that A begins to light regularly.

The significance of explanatory asymmetry in deciding causal asymmetry becomes more illuminating when we suppose that, as a further modification to the example, upon being connected to the switch the two bulbs are somehow synchronized such that B begins to light randomly, in a way that is exactly like A. In this case, I contend that, again in the light of explanatory priority, it is A's lighting a certain colour that causes B to light that colour too, rather than the other way around. It is interesting to notice that, in the new scenario the correlation between A's lighting and B's lightings is, *in itself*, indistinguishable from that in the original example. In the original example, it is also the case that A and B, when both connected to the switch, light randomly, and somehow in a same way. But, as we have seen, it is not possible to tell the cause from the effect in the original example. The reason it couldn't be done then but can be done now, obviously, is that in the modified version of the example an explanatory asymmetry is introduced—B does not light randomly before being connected to the switch together with A, and consequently its newly obtained random lighting can be explained by reference to that of A's, but the reverse does not hold.[54]

---

[54] If this discussion is correct, then the thesis according to which causation is an intrinsic relation cannot be totally right. Taking events as causal relata, what the thesis of intrinsicness of causation says is basically that two events are causally

So the causal asymmetry between A and B's same lightings becomes intelligible only after we take into consideration some explanatory factors about their lightings. If it is possible to make sense of one the lightings as explanatory prior to the other, it is then possible to identify the former as the cause and the latter the effect. Note that I am not suggesting that the explanatory asymmetry is merely *evidence* of the causal asymmetry. Rather, my view is that explanatory asymmetry *is* causal asymmetry. In the original setting of the example, where A and B light randomly but in the same way, it is not just that we don't know which causes which. Rather, the point is that in that setting it makes little sense to say which causes which. By comparison, in the modified setting, where B comes to light randomly

---

related, only in virtue of the properties and relations of the two events themselves and not due to anything independent of these properties and relations. (For a discussion of this thesis, see Menzies [1999] and Hall [2004a].) In our example, it appears problematic to say that in the original setting A's lighting causes B's lighting, or vice versa, but right to say that in the modified setting A's lighting causes B's lighting. This is so, despite the fact that the two settings are *intrinsically indistinguishable*.

and thus its random lighting is in need of explanation, it then becomes intelligible to say that A's lighting a certain colour causes B to light that colour too.

Put generally, the point is that in order to make sense of the causal asymmetry between two causally related simultaneous events we have to resort to the explanatory asymmetry between them. This point becomes even more important in making sense of the cause-effect distinction in putative cases of backwards causation, a topic I shall now turn to.

3.3 Backwards Causation

If the notion of simultaneous causation sounds questionable, the notion of backwards causation sounds just bizarre. First of all, we do not seem to encounter any cases of backwards causation, in which an event L can be plausibly said to cause an earlier event E. But even the conceptual possibility of backwards causation seems to be in great doubt. How could L, which has not been yet, cause an earlier E, which has already been? Incredible as the idea of backwards causation appears to be, mainly due to Michael Dummett's seminal works from the mid-1950s and thereafter, there have been many interesting discussions on this topic. Of course, not every issue related to this topic needs to be addressed. I shall only in this section focus on the question of which factor, in some suggested scenarios of backwards causation, decisively determines a cause-effect distinction that is in favour of this special conception of causation. In particular, I shall be largely concentrating upon the so-called 'bilking' argument, which has been widely employed to block some major attempts to validate the notion of backwards causation. In the course of the discussion, my main point about causal asymmetry will be made.

Before getting into the details of the bilking argument, I want to briefly set aside three issues about backwards causation: two controversial issues that I will set aside, and one easy issue that I will not put too much weight on. First, in his discussion of basic actions, i.e., actions that an agent cannot perform by doing something else, von Wright [1971: 77] suggests that 'by performing basic actions we bring about earlier events in our neural system'. The idea is that, for example, whenever I raise my arm (this is supposed to be a basic action), a corresponding neural event N occurs in my brain. Usually we think that N must occur slightly before my arm-raising, so as to give rise to the latter. However, according to von Wright, there is a sense in which we can say that my arm-raising causes N, but not the other way around: by raising my arm I can *bring about* N, but it is not the case that I can bring about my arm-raising by bringing about N. N, the neural event, seems not to be subject to my direct control. Rather, it seems that the only way I can bring about N is simply by performing the basic action of raising my arm. If this is the case, backwards causation becomes quite common—in performing a basic action the agent thereby causes an earlier neural event to occur.

It is not hard to see that there are some serious problems with von Wright's case. For one thing, as mentioned in the Introduction, the manipulative theory of causation, on which his case of backwards causation is clearly based, suffers heavily from circularity. Even though the fact that by bringing about A we could bring about B may *indicate* that A causes B, this does not mean that we can understand this bringing-about relation without presupposing the causal relation. For another thing, it seems wrong to say without qualification that the arm-raising cannot be brought about by bringing about N. A neurophysiologist, as von Wright also agrees, may manage to do this to her subject. In order to make a distinction between the everyday case where one's arm-raising causes N and the neurophysiologist case where on the contrary N causes one's arm-raising, von Wright has to maintain that there are correspondingly two different 'closed systems'. In one closed system, my arm-raising causes N; in another, rather the opposite is the case. At this point, however, Mackie comments:

> It is very tempting to say that on an occasion when I actually raise my arm, so that by von Wright's account the neural events are the effect, they are causally prior in that a neurophysiologist *could have* interfered with them and could *thereby* have prevented my arm from rising ... if the neurophysiologist could have brought about not-q by suppressing p, then p was in fact causally prior to q, and it would then be contradictory to say that since I actually brought about p by doing q, q was also in fact causally prior to p. [1974: 172]

I agree. It seems that the problem pointed out by Mackie, as well as the general problem with von Wright's manipulative theory of causation, is not easy to resolve.

So I suggest that we set aside von Wright's dubious case of backwards causation.

The second issue I want to set aside is time travel. Obviously, if time travel to the past is logically if not physically possible, then we have an easy case of backwards causation. A time traveller's enjoying her good-bye dinner, for example, may cause her to feel full of energy when she steps out her time machine in the past. But the issue of time travel is rather complicated and controversial, and better to be avoided too. It is better just to concentrate on some more conventional scenarios in which the notion of backwards causation may be said to make sense.

Third, I take it to be a relatively easy issue that backwards causation is conceivable in an *agent-free* world. In his classic paper, Dummett [1964] asks us to consider a world in which all causal processes seem to occur in reverse, and think about what we, merely as observers but not agents in that world, have to say in that scenario. His contention is:

> [In such a world] we should have great difficulty
> in arriving at causal explanations that accounted
> for events in terms of the processes which had

led up to them. The sapling grows gradually smaller, finally reducing itself to an apple pip; then an apple is gradually constituted around the pip from ingredients found in the soil; at a certain moment the apple rolls along the ground, gradually gaining momentum, bounces a few times, and then suddenly takes off vertically and attached itself with a snap to the bough of an apple tree. Viewed from the standpoint of gross observation, this process contains many totally unpredictable elements: we cannot, for example, explain, by reference to the conditions obtaining at the moment when the apple started rolling, why it started rolling at that moment or in that direction. Rather, we should have to substitute a system of explanations of events in terms of the processes that led back to them from some subsequent moment … we can conceive of a world in which a notion of causality associated with the opposite direction would have been more appropriate and, so long as we consider ourselves as mere observers of such a world, there is no particular conceptual difficulty about the

conception of such a backwards causation.
[1964: 339-40]

It is easy to see that in arguing for the conceivability of backwards causation, insofar as it occurs in a scenario in which no human agent is involved, Dummett appeals to the later cause-factor's explanatory power, as opposed to the earlier effect-factor's lack of that power. In the world he imagines, it appears right to regard, say, the apple's rolling in a certain direction as caused by its later bouncing, but not the other way around. This is so, because by reference to the latter we can explain the former, whereas the reverse does not hold. Apparently, Dummett's view about the cause-effect distinction—although he is only concerned with this distinction in case of backwards causation—is quite compatible with my own view about casual asymmetry. (I agree with him that, in cases of backwards causation, a later event can be regarded as causing an earlier one, insofar as by reference to the former the latter can be explained, in a way the latter cannot be said to explain the former. More generally, my view is that, whether for backwards causation or

Borderline Cases (I)

for any other kinds of causation, causal asymmetry simply consists in a certain explanatory asymmetry.)

Having said that backwards causation is conceivable in a world devoid of agent-intervention, the situation is much more complicated once this kind of intervention is introduced. As an immediate rejoinder to Dummett's initial attempt [1954] to make sense of the notion of backwards causation, Flew [1954] came up with a counter-argument, which was from then on labelled after the term he used as 'the bilking argument', and has become a popular means of rejecting backwards causation. It is not easy to present the argument in a straightforward way though, as it has been elaborated by many philosophers, in more or less different and not necessarily compatible ways[55]. Here is a first approximation of the basic idea of the argument. Suppose someone suggests that an event L causes an earlier event E.[56] It

---

[55] It has been formulated, among others, in Flew [1954, 1956, 1957], Black [1956], Pears [1957], Mellor [1981], Oddie [1990], Tooley [1997], Ben-Yani [2007].

[56] This suggestion makes initial sense, it should be noted, only on a couple of conditions. First, there are good reasons to deny that E causes L; second, L is caused by factors that are causally

would then be possible for us, at least in principle, after observing E's occurrence, to try to prevent L from occurring. But in trying to do so we would face a dilemma:

> (1) One the one hand, if we succeed in the prevention, the stipulated causal connection between L and E would be broken down, since that would be a situation in which E occurs without L's occurrence, a situation in which L is not causally effective in making E occur.
>
> (2) If, on the other hand, once E has occurred we somehow simply could not prevent L

---

independent of E; and third, E has no earlier sufficient cause. Here is an example in which arguably these conditions hold: a disaster was precisely predicted by some honest man who unconsciously uttered the prediction upon waking up from deep sleep all of sudden (the idea is that the disaster caused him to make the prediction). Whether this is a real case of backwards causation is not my concern. I give this example, only to show that there are certain conditions needed to make it a *prima facie* case of backwards causation.

from occurring, this would show that L itself is not independent of E, and it may even be argued on this ground that, far from being the case that L caused E, the converse is more likely to be true.

One thing unsatisfactory about this formulation of the bilking argument is that it makes the argument seem to merely, but unfairly, focus on *a single case* of backwards causation. Actually, few advocates of the notion of backwards causation would suggest that the backwards causal relation from L to E can be made intelligible merely by considering this single case. Rather, the suggestion is that the putative causal relation from L to E makes sense, provided that there is an observed correlation between L-type events (for short, L-events) and E-type events (E-events). The primary reason we want to say that L backwardly caused E is not just that their single co-occurrence is observed, but that this *kind* of co-occurrence has been regularly observed.[57] Therefore, the

---

[57] Obviously, this point reflects an element of truth contained in the regularity theory of causation.

bilking argument will not gain its full force unless it can be in some way modified so as to be applicable to a general causal relation between L-events and E-events.

Another thing is that even if we can often bring about situations in which E-events occur without L-events, this appears not to be a problem for those who regard a cause, given certain circumstances and laws of nature, as a *sufficient* condition for its effect. Anyway, even with regard to normal forward causal relations we do not always require that cause-events[58] are necessary for the effect-events, or that the cause-events have to occur on every occasion where the effect-events occur. No one would say, for example, if I once had a fever without catching cold then it (i.e., a fever of a same type) can never be caused by my catching cold (i.e., a catching of cold of a same type). So even if on some, or even most, occasions, E-events occur without L-events, this does not provide conclusive support for rejecting the idea that a *particular* L, as a sufficient condition of E, can still be regarded as a cause of E. There seems to be an easy way out of this difficulty though. In addition to saying that we

---

[58] Here when I say 'cause-events' I mean cause-events of a same type; same to 'effect-events'.

can prevent L-events despite the occurrence of E-events, a clause can be inserted into the bilking argument as saying that we can also get L-events to occur without E-events. Thus the stipulation that L-events are sufficient causes of E-events will be ruled out.[59]

Based on these considerations I suggest that the bilking argument be modified as follows. Suppose someone suggests that L-events cause earlier E-events. It is then possible for us, at least in principle, both

> (*i*) after observing E-events' presence, to try to prevent L-events from occurring;
>
> *and*
>
> (*ii*) after observing E-events' absence, to try to make L-events occur.

---

[59] Pears [1957: 83] pointed out the problem we discussed in this paragraph; Oddie [1990: 99] accordingly made the modification to the bilking argument.

One who thinks that L-events cause E-events faces the following dilemma in both cases:

> Dilemma-*i*: On the one hand, if, in the presence of E-events, we succeed in preventing L-events, any view that takes L-events to be *necessary*[60] causes of E-events will be undermined, since there will be a situation in which E-events occur without L-events. If, on the other hand, once E-events have occurred we somehow simply cannot prevent L-events from occurring, this will show that L-events are actually not independent of E-events, and it may even be argued on this ground that, far from it being the case that L-events cause E-events, the converse is more likely to be true.

> Dillemma-*ii*: On the one hand, if, in the absence of E-events, we succeed in bringing about L-events, any view that takes L-events to be *sufficient* causes of E-events will be undermined,

---

[60] This is in the sense of their being 'without-which-not', not 'not-possibly-not', a distinction made clear in Mellor [1995: 16].

since there will be a situation in which E-events fail to occur in spite of the occurrence of L-events'. If, on the other hand, once E-events have failed to occur we somehow simply cannot bring about L-events, this will show that L-events' are not independent of E-events, and it may even be argued on this ground that, far from it being the case that L-events cause E-events, the converse is more likely to be true.

Unfortunately, the bilking argument thus formulated is still not fully satisfactory. In particular, this formulation assumes that we as agents are able to prevent certain events, as well as bring them about, and that when we cannot do these things there must be some factors *external to ourselves as agents* that make it so. These assumptions are debatable, and go deep into the metaphysics of agency. At any rate, it seems that the proponent of the notion of backwards causation may argue that to understand a world of backwards causation we have adopt a special view about agency. But I aim to examine an internal problem with the bilking argument, so shall set aside issues about agency and, for the sake of argument, grant that our conception of agency is just what the bilking argument assumes.

What interests me is the second horn(s) of the dilemma(s) in the bilking argument. Take for example the second horn in Dilemma-*i*. What it says is that in cases where E-events occur, and where we try but somehow always fail to prevent L-events, it must be that L-events are not independent of E-events, and it may even be argued on this ground that, far from being the case that L-events cause E-events, the converse is more likely to be true. More precisely, the idea is this: suppose that we as agents have the usual power to suppress L-events, unless of course some other causal factors external to us effectively prevent us from doing so. When we find out that we cannot suppress L-events, the 'inevitability' of L-events thus needs an *explanation*. In the context, it seems that an obvious option for this explanation is to say that E-events, which have already occurred, cause it to be the case that L-events become inevitable. So the inevitability of L-events can be explained by appeal to the notion of forward causation we usually employ. (Likewise, with respect to the second horn in Dilemma-*ii*, in cases where E-events do not occur, and where we try but somehow always fail to bring L-events about, the same explanation, *mutatis mutandis*, will apply.)

But the interesting point is that the above explanation of the inevitability of L-events is not the only plausible explanation we can manage to give in the scenario under discussion. From a different point of view, isn't it that, we cannot suppress L-events, simply because they are *causes* of E-events and, as long as E-events occur, their causes, L-events, have to occur?[61] For any causal connection, it seems that if the cause occurs, the effect does not have to occur—the causal process may be interrupted, anyway. By contrast, given that the effect occurs, it seems that the cause has to occur—otherwise the effect would be gratuitous. In light of this explanation, not only does the second horn fail to shed doubt on the notion of backward causation, but it actually renders support to it.

Some may become impatient and ask: Which, as between E-events and L-events, are causes and which are effects anyway? You first tell us that E-events can be plausibly regarded as causes and L-events effects, and then tell us that the opposite is also plausible. What is

---

[61] This point is brought to my attention by David Oderberg.

your point? The point is that there is no *unconditional* answer to the question raised about the causal status of E-events and L-events. And—this is pertinent to my overall view about causal asymmetry—the condition required here is a certain *explanatory interest*. In the putative scenarios of backwards causation, if we focus on explaining the inevitability of L-events, it makes more sense to say that E-events are the causes and L-events the effects; if, instead, we focus on explaining the very existence of E-events, it makes more sense to say that L-events are the causes and E-events the effects.[62] In such scenarios, a shift in our explanatory focus immediately results in a shift of our understanding the causal asymmetry. Our analysis of the bilking argument, then, again supports the view that causal asymmetry consists in explanatory asymmetry.

---

[62] No doubt, in the latter case it can always be wondered whether E-events may actually be caused by some unidentified causal antecedents. But the putative scenarios of backwards causation are puzzling, partly because, *ex hypothesi*, there are no such causal antecedents of E-events stipulated in the scenarios. See Note 9 (this chapter).

Chapter 4

Borderline Cases (II): Absence Causation

4.1 Introduction

4.2 Non-relational Causation

4.3 Absences as Existents

4.4 Causation and Causal Explanation

4.1 Introduction

For the view that causation is always a relation absences, or omissions[63], pose a problem. A relation needs relata.

---

[63] The notion of omission has a connotation closely associated with *action*, which is not my concern. I only talk about absences in general.

But it seems that absences by their nature simply do not exist, and so cannot be related, let alone be causally related. However, it can hardly be denied that, at least on the face of it, absences can sometimes cause and be caused. For example, Leo's vacation in China causes his failing to water his flower back in the UK, which in turn causes it to die. Leo's failing to water the flower, as an absence of his watering it, seems to have causal antecedents as well as consequents. The problem faced by those who regard causation as a relation, therefore, is how to make sense of causal relations that apparently take absences as relata.

To facilitate diagnosis, however, the problem needs to be formulated more rigorously. We have just described the problem in effect as a discrepancy between a seemingly plausible argument against the notion of absence causation on the one hand, and a commonsense conviction of that notion on the other. The argument against absence causation, which may be called the argument from existent relata, runs as follows:

(1) Causation is a relation;

(2) A relation needs relata;

(3) Non-existents cannot be relata for any relation;

(4) Absences are non-existents.

Therefore,

(5) There cannot be absence causation, in which absences are causes or effects.

This conclusion is at odds with our commonsense disposition to regard absences, such as Leo's not watering his flower or the like, as causes and effects. According to the common understanding, the following claim appears to be true:

(6) There are cases of absence causation, in which absences are causes or effects.

Facing (5) and (6) we are then in a dilemma; this dilemma is what I call the problem of absence causation. Obviously, the problem can be avoid by denying either (5) or (6); and (5) in turn loses support if any of its premises from (1) to (4) turns out to be false.

This way of setting out the problem, however, is unnecessarily strong. About (1), (4) and (6) I will say more in detail. (2) appears to be analytically true, and can be set aside. What seems dubious is (3), according to which non-existents cannot be relata for *any* relation. But, anyway, it appears that when I say I love Santa Claus what I mean is partly that there is a love-relation from me towards Santa, even though Santa, as a matter of fact, does not exist. Sure enough, it may be pointed out that the relation of love, interpreted as an *intentional* relation, need not entail the existence of what is loved. I may love, envy, or indeed disbelieve in Santa without there being such a man as Santa. But still it remains plausible to say that a *causal* relation, by contrast, has to be existence-entailing on both sides of the relation. So for example if it is the case that I *quarrelled* with my grandpa—unlike the case that I love him—then there had to be me, and there had to be my grandpa. The question of to what extent relations other than causation are existence-entailing is an interesting one on its own, but need not detain us here.[64] The point I want to press here is that in order to make the argument from existent relata go through, there is no need to take (3), a general claim about the existence status of all relata in all sorts of relations, as one of its premises. To do so will only make the argument unnecessarily strong, and as a result vulnerable to various counterexamples. It will suffice for the purpose of the argument to avoid talking about relations in general, but say instead that causal relations *in particular* cannot admit non-existents as relata. This claim, though weaker, is a more plausible premise for the argument.

In light of this, let us then reformulate the problem of absence causation. To begin with, there is an argument from existent *causal* relata showing that there cannot be absence causation:

---

[64] See Bigelow [1996] for an able discussion on this issue.

(i) Causation is a relation;

(ii) A causal relation cannot admit non-existents as relata;

(iii) Absences are non-existents.

Therefore,

(iv) There cannot be absence causation, in which absences are causes or effects.

But, contra (iv), according to commonsense,

(v) There are cases of absence causation, in which absences are causes or effects.

It seems to me that the argument from existent causal relata, as it stands, is valid. I have conceded (ii) to be plausible, and will not attempt to challenge the argument by challenging (ii). In what follows I will first examine some possible ways in which (i) or (iii) may be put into question, ways that upon reflection turn out to be unsound. Second, I will move on to a proposed rejection of (v), a rejection that, though it contains considerable truth, needs to be re-interpreted in the light of my proposed general view about the relation between causation and explanation.

4.2 Non-relational Causation

So to claim (i). It may appear at first glance that (i)—i.e., causation is a relation—is a conceptual truth. If there are only a few things we can be sure about causation, isn't one that causation is a relation? Not so, perhaps, in face of the problem of absence causation. It is easy to see that in order to solve the problem as it has been formulated, one may choose to deny (i), that causation is a relation (or at least that causation is *always* a relation), as long as one wants to maintain (ii), (iii) and (v). David Lewis follows this line of thinking, and his response to the problem of absence causation is as follows:

> The best response is to concede that a void is nothing at all, and that a lesser absence is nothing relevant at all and therefore cannot furnish causal relata. Yet absences can be causes and effects. So I insist ... that causation cannot always be the bearing of a causal relation. No theory of the causal relation ... can be the whole story of causation. [Lewis 2004b: 282]

Essential to Lewis' response is the view that a distinction should be made between *causation* and a *causal relation*[65]. According to this distinction, even though absences cannot be causally related (because, it is said, they are nothing and thus cannot furnish causal relata), somehow they can still be causes and effects in some kind of non-relational causation. To what extent this distinction makes sense I will say more shortly.

---

[65] As noted before (Ch. 2, Note 24) Lewis also made another distinction between *causation* and *causal dependence* (in the literature the latter is sometime also called 'causal relation'). This distinction is made in order to ensure transitivity of causation, and is irrelevant here.

But, as a first impression, Lewis' distinction may appear to be philosophically uninteresting. It appears as if he made the distinction between causation and causal relations, simply to accommodate the common-sense view that absences can be causes and effects.[66] This looks similar to someone's making, say, a distinction between intentional lies and unintentional ones, simply to make room for some dubious cases of unintentional 'lies' that are somehow endorsed by the majority of people. Presumably this is a bad way to make sense of the notion of an unintentional lie. For, without offering any argument, those who take some unintentional false assertions to be lies are very likely confused about what a lie really is. In the same way, it seems to be as bad to make sense of the notion of absence causation, simply by uncritically following people to call it 'causation', and artificially differentiating it from 'causal relation'. Why cannot common parlance be wrong, and we deny that absences ever cause or are caused?

---

[66] It appears so, particularly when he says that '[s]imply to state this response [i.e., a response to the problem of absence causation by saying that absences never cause anything] is to complete the reductio against it' [2004b: 281].

The point, however, is that Lewis has a more philosophical reason to support his view that absences, albeit unsuitable for being causal relata, can be causes and effects. The view is said to be in harmony with his counterfactual analysis of causation. And this is how:

> If the cause is an absence, then to suppose away the cause counterfactually is not to attend to some remarkable entity and suppose that it does *not* exist. Rather, we need only suppose that some *un*remarkable entity *does* exist. Absences are spooky things, and we'd do best not to take them seriously. But absences of absences are no problem. [2004b: 282-3]

Take the Leo example. The idea is that even though Leo's not watering his flower, as an absence, is too spooky an entity to be causally related, the counterfactual 'If he had watered the flower[67], it would not have died' makes perfect sense. Generally speaking, the supposition of the

---

[67] More precisely, this is to say 'if a watering of the flower by him had occurred'.

nonexistence of an absence (i.e., the supposition of a presence) is the supposition that a bona fide entity does exist and thus the supposition can be taken as the antecedent of a certain counterfactual conditional. Provided that we regard counterfactual dependence as a reliable test for causation, it seems to follow that the absence can be a cause. Likewise, an absence can also be maintained to be an effect. The fact that absences fit well into patterns of counterfactual dependence thus vindicates the view that there are cases of absence causation. On the other hand, considering the fact (as Lewis sees it) that absences can in no way be causal relata, so-called absence causation must not be understood as a causal relation. Hence a distinction between causation and causal relation is required, and room is made for absence causation.

However, Lewis' distinction between causation and causal relation, and for that matter his denial of causation to be always a relation, is far from satisfactory. Even worse, his discussion leaves the impression that he is not quite clear about the distinction he tries to make. It seems that Lewis has three different kinds of thing in mind: causation, causal pairs (cause and effect), and causal relations. While he always maintains that absence causation is a kind of causation, and always denies that absences can ever be causally related, some ambivalence is shown when he tries to decide whether absences can be causes and effects. At several places [2000: 195; 2004a: 99-100; 2004b: 282] he is quite confident in saying that absences can be causes and effects, but shows in another place [2004a: 100] considerable reluctance in doing so, and says instead that 'when an absence is a cause or an effect, there is *strictly speaking* [my italics] nothing at all that is a cause or effect'. I take this indecisiveness as a symptom of the fact that he is trying to make a distinction where there is actually none. Understandably, Lewis wants to say that absences can be causes and effects, since presumably absences' being causes and effects is what absence causation, the notion of which he accepts as part of common sense, is all about. But if absences can be causes and effects, it seems to follow immediately that they have to be, qua being causes and effects, causally related. How can there possibly be any other way in which two entities can be cause and effect except by their being related as cause and effect? Yet Lewis firmly holds that absences cannot be causal relata. So he has to admit that absences, after all, cannot be causes and effects. But this is inconsistent. It is hard to see what Lewis means when he says that when an absence is a cause or effect, strictly speaking nothing is a cause or effect (this 'strictly speaking' sounds to me like an 'illogically speaking'!). I suggest that we do better by sticking to the conceptual truth that causation is indeed a relation. If absences can be related as causes and effects then there can be absence causation; if not, not; and that is that. Besides challenging the obvious, there must be more plausible ways to deal with the problem of absence causation.

But even if we reject Lewis' distinction between causation and causal relation as unclear, the question remains as to how to make sense of the fact that absences do fit into patterns of counterfactual dependence fairly smoothly. Are we compelled to say that, although absences cannot be causes and effects, let alone be causally related (suppose this is in some sense different from their being causes and effects), still they must figure in causation, insofar as they fit well into patterns of counterfactual dependence? Well, this suggestion may sound misleading to those who do not endorse the counterfactual analysis of causation. If the counterfactual analysis is wrong, or essentially inadequate, then of course there is no need to find a place for absences in causation simply because they fit into patterns of counterfactual dependence. Anyway, there are cases of non-causal counterfactual dependence.[68] And absences may be involved in a kind of non-causal counterfactual dependence without being involved in causation. But let us for the sake of argument suppose that the counterfactual analysis is essentially correct. Suppose, according to the standard counterfactual analysis [Lewis 1986], that counterfactual dependence between wholly distinct *events* is sufficient for causation. So event c causes event e, if it is true that had c not occurred, e would not have had occurred. Now, since Lewis [2000: 195; 2004b: 281] does not regard absences as events, obviously he cannot say that an absence gets involved in causation in the way that c or e does. Rather, his suggestion is that an absence gets involved in causation, as far as a *negative existential proposition* that states the absence enters into patterns of counterfactual dependence.[69] The idea, as far as I can tell, is that an absence gets involved in causation, not as an event, but only as a *negative fact* that no event of a certain

---

[68] See Kim [1973b]

[69] As Lewis [2000: 195-6] makes it clearly, 'it is by way of just such propositions [negative existential propositions that absences occur], and only by way of such propositions, that absences enter into patterns of counterfactual dependence.'

type occurs. So even though Leo's not watering his flower is not an event, it can be said that the fact that he did not water the flower causes the flower's death, because the counterfactual 'If it had not been the case that he did not the flower, the flower would not have died' is true.

To regard absences as negative facts so as to get around the problem of absence causation is an option I will discuss separately. For Lewis, however, I doubt that he can be fully happy with this solution. Even though there seems to be no serious problem in modifying the counterfactual analysis of causation to admit facts, as well as events, as causal relata, Lewis [2004a: 100; 2004b: 289] appears to have a strong distaste for the idea that facts can be taken as causal relata. His reason is that we should distinguish between a cause (or an effect) itself and a true proposition—that is, according to him, a fact[70]—that describes it. The causal work is done by events, not propositions.

But even if one is happy with the solution that an absence as a negative fact enters into patterns of counterfactual dependence and thus to that extent causes and is

---

[70] We will return to this point in next section.

caused, still there is another difficulty for this kind of counterfactual analysis of absence causation. The difficulty, as discussed by Beebee [2004] and McGrath [2005], is that a counterfactual analysis of absence causation not only often gets things right, but also, more often indeed, gets things wrong. According to commonsense, not only do we want to say that Leo's not watering the flower caused it to die, but we also want to *deny* that, say, the Queen's not watering the flower, or Lewis' not watering the flower, also caused it to die. But if we adopt the counterfactual analysis, the commonsense differentiation can hardly be respected. This is so, obviously because the counterfactual 'If it had not been the case that the Queen did not water the flower, it would not have died' is true, as much as the counterfactual 'If it had not been the case that Leo did not water the flower, it would not have died'. Admittedly, one may insist, in line with Lewis [2000: 196; 2004a: 101], that it is an ontological truth that the Queen's not watering the flower did cause its death, even though in most circumstances and for pragmatic reasons we do not feel obliged to utter this truth. But this position is untenable. Note that Lewis also notoriously insists that one's birth is a cause of one's death, for the same reason that the two events fit into

Borderline Cases (II)

patterns of counterfactual dependence. About the birth case he might be right.[71] But, as McGrath [op. cit.: 129] points out, the birth case is different from the non-watering case or any other case of absence, in that in the latter, but not the former, not only do we refrain from asserting certain causal truths, but we also assert certain causal falsehoods (that is, falsehoods according to the counterfactual analysis of absence causation). Even if it is granted that for pragmatic reasons we do not always want to assert the causal truth that one's birth caused his death, we do not merely not wish to assert that the Queen's not watering the flower caused its death; we actually wish to *deny* this. The fact is not tacitly compatible with the counterfactual analysis; rather, it is *incompatible* with the analysis. For those who are not already disposed to accept the counterfactual analysis, this incompatibility clearly indicates that the counterfactual analysis is inadequate, at least in the case of absence causation.

To sum up my criticism of Lewis' approach, Lewis makes a distinction between causation and causal relations, by way of which he denies that causation is always a relation. If the distinction stands, on the one

---

[71] He is not though. We will see why in next chapter.

hand he can endorse absence causation, and on the other hand deny that absences can be causally related. We have seen, however, that the proposed distinction does not make much sense. What backs up Lewis' intuition that there must be absence causation is that absences fit into patterns of counterfactual dependence, and this, according to his counterfactual analysis of causation, is sufficient to conclude that absence causation exists. But even if the counterfactual analysis as a general theory of causation is acceptable (which I doubt[72]), as far as absences are concerned it cannot always get things right. Indeed it more often gets things wrong, in cases where intuitively we want to deny, but the counterfactual analysis sanctions, the claim that there are certain causal relations. I conclude, therefore, that in dealing with the problem of absence causation Lewis' distinction between causation and causal relation and for that matter his denial that causation is always a relation will not do.

---

[72] In Ch. 2.4 we discussed some reason for this doubt.

4.3 Absences as Existents

Another way to solve the problem of absence causation is to challenge premise (iii) of the argument from existent causal relata, i.e., the claim that absences are non-existents. Indeed, the claim may strike us as vague. What kind of non-existents are we talking about? Since there are different kinds of existence, absences denied one kind of existence may possess another. Instead of asking whether absences can exist, simplciter, the more meaningful question one should ask is 'As what can absences exist?'

One thing at least we can get intuitively right is that an absence cannot exist as an object (by this I mean a substance). An object exists independently from any other and arguably independently of any particular properties, but an absence, if existent at all, surely cannot exist in this way. An absence is always an absence *of* something, no matter whether this 'something' is an object, or a property. In light of this, a more plausible way to think about an absence is to think about it more or less as a Kimian triple [1973a][73]: an entity such that it is the

---

[73] Kim himself didn't discuss absences as such triples.

absence of an object, and/or the absence of a property of the object, and/or the object's exemplification of the property *not* at a certain (period of) time.[74] So for example Leo's not watering the flower may be written as '([Leo, t], ¬watering the flower)', which can be roughly read as Leo's having a negative property of not watering the flower at t. Or maybe the triple in question should be rather in the form of ([¬Leo, t], watering the flower), or ([Leo, ¬t], watering the flower), or various other combinations of the negation of Leo, the negation of watering the flower, and the negation of the time t.[75] These tricky questions need not detain us though. The important point

---

[74] For simplicity here we negelect multiple objects or multiple properties (relations).

[75] No doubt, a Kimian triple involving negative constitutives appears to be a tricky entity. For one thing, it seems hard to tell whether ([Leo, t], ¬watering the flower) is actually identical with ([¬Leo, t], watering the flower), or maybe even with ([¬Leo, ¬t], ¬watering the flower). Our thought on this kind of questions may easily go astray, and I suggest we better leave them aside. At any rate, my view, as will become clear shortly, is that absences are not events. So if construing an absence as a Kimian triple is a problematic, my view will not be shaken, but rather be strengthened.

Borderline Cases (II)

is that since a Kimian triple is supposed to be an event[76], we may, as a first attempt, regard an absence as an event. This approach is attractive, especially if, as far as causation is concerned, we want to remain faithful to the doctrine of event causation. According to this doctrine, the initial difficulty for the notion of absence causation can be posed by saying that since absences are not events (rather, they are the lack of events), and given that only events can be causally related, absences cannot be causes or effects. To get around this difficulty, a simple but, if successful, very effective move is to suggest that absences are indeed events—of a special kind, but events nevertheless. More explicitly, the suggestion is that although absences are not positive events, they are *negative* ones, which still exist in some sense[77]. On this view, while Leo's watering the flower is a positive event, his not doing so is a negative one. And just as his

---

[76] Bennett [1988, esp. Ch. 5] does not think so. He thinks that a Kimian triple is a fact, not an event. I don't have to take side on this issue, since I will later on consider absences as facts anyway.

[77] Usually we say that objects exist but events occur. This difference is immaterial in what follows. I will use 'existence' and 'occurrence' of an event interchangeably.

watering the flower has causes and effects, so does his not watering it.

In the literature on events few have taken seriously the idea of a negative event.[78] The reason behind this may be that a negative event, because it is negative, it is somehow thought to be nowhere and no-when. Since all events proper have to be spatiotemporally located, the so-called negative events falling short of this requirement must not be genuine events. But this reason does not stand up to scrutiny. Even though Leo's not watering the flower is problematic with respect to its spatiotemporal location (is it around his seat in his return flight to UK and during the time of the flight, or rather along the Chang'an Street in Beijing where he did a walking tour and during the time of the tour?), presumably in this respect it is not more problematic than some otherwise bona fide positive events, such as a war, or an economic recession. While it is admittedly hard to tell where and when Leo's not watering the flower happened *exactly*, it appears hard to tell where and when the Great Depression

---

[78] Chisholm [1970] and Peterson [1989] are two exceptions. But they mentioned, and made use of the notion of a negative event, much more than argued for it.

Borderline Cases (II)

happened *exactly* as well. (Is the depression on Wall Street, or on the dinner table of a Detroit worker's family, or both, or neither? Is it from 1930 until 1933, or lasting throughout 1930s? And if it is until 1933, does it disappear second by second along with the descending of the Time Square New Year's Eve Ball?) The spatiotemporal location of many positive events is very problematic too, but this by itself does not prevent us from acknowledging that there are such events. So we have no justification has been provided for a bias in favour of positive events.

In order to show that there cannot be such a thing as a negative event we need a stronger argument. Mellor [1995: 133-4] offers one. As his argument is related to the development of our discussion in more than one way, it deserves a close look.

Mellor begins his argument by considering an entailment between propositions about positive events. To stick with our own example, 'Leo watered the flower quickly' entails 'Leo watered the flower', since obviously nothing can be both quick and a flower-watering without being a flower-watering.[79] By contrast, for negative

---

[79] Obviously, Mellor is inspired by Davidson's discussion of adverbial modification. According to Davidson [1980], the

propositions the entailment goes in the opposite direction. 'Leo did not water the flower' entails 'Leo did not water the flower quickly', since if he did not water the flower, then of course he did not water it quickly. Now, the point is that 'Leo did not water the flower' also entails 'Leo did not water the flower *slowly*'. So if we suppose that 'Leo did not water the flower' is made true by a negative event, namely his not watering the flower, then we have to conclude that this negative event has two contrary

---

reason we should admit events into our ontology is that without doing so we cannot make sense of a commonly accepted inference involving the dropping of adverbs in English sentences about events. We all know that from the sentence 'Jones buttered the toast slowly at midnight' it follows 'Jones buttered the toast slowly', from which it in turn follows 'Jones buttered the toast'. Davidson contends that the best way to understand this kind of inference is to quantify over events (or actions, which are supposed to be a species of events). Roughly, the idea is that if we read the sentence 'Jones buttered the toast slowly at midnight' as saying that there was an event such that it was a buttering, and Jones was its subject, and the toast was its object, and it was slow, and it was at midnight, then to infer by dropping these conjuncts become a simple matter of applying the rule of 'simplification' in first order logic.

properties, namely both being quick and being slow. But this is impossible. So the putative negative event, Leo's not watering the flower, does not exist.

One might raise two objections to Mellor's argument (which he himself didn't consider). Both, however, are untenable. To start with, some may point out that properties like being quick or being slow are not applicable to negative events. Anyway, negative events are of a special kind, and it should not be too surprising if they do not admit of properties that are usually applied to positive events. Note that this consideration is not as ad hoc as it appears to be. Even for positive events, or indeed positive objects, a property can sometimes be misapplied. Suppose that someone says that Michael Jackson's music is red, would we then argue, along Mellor's line, that since his music is also green and being green is incompatible with being red, there must be no such thing as Jackson's music? Of course we wouldn't. Here, the correct thing to say is that being red, as well as being green, is simply not applicable to Jackson's music in the first place. In the same way, it may be urged, the correct thing to say about the alleged being quick or being slow of Leo's not watering the flower is that the two properties are not applicable to the non-watering. If so, Mellor's argument becomes a non-starter.

This objection, however, misunderstands the point of Mellor's argument. According to Mellor, it is not as if we can just arbitrarily *assign* a pair of incompatible properties to a given negative event, and conclude that the event must not exist. If that were the idea of Mellor's argument, it would indeed be effective in disproving the existence of everything—Jackson's music, Big Ben, World Cup 2010, etc—to be existent. The World Cup 2010, for example, may be assigned as being won by North Korea, as well as the property of being won by England. Since the two properties had by this World Cup, being won by North Korea and being won by England, are incompatible with each other, we can therefore conclude that there must be no such a thing as World Cup 2010! This is absurd, obviously because the assignment of either of the two properties is groundless to begin with. Unlike the case of the World Cup 2010 or Jackson's music, however, the idea of Mellor's argument is that we do have good reason to say that a pair of incompatible properties such as being quick and being slow are both applicable to Leo's not watering the flower as a negative event. The reason, as explained before, is that from 'Leo did not water the

Borderline Cases (II)

flower' it entails 'Leo did not water the flower quickly', as well as 'Leo did not water the flower slowly'. So if we think that the first proposition is made true by Leo's not watering the flower as a negative event, it seems reasonable to think that the second proposition is made true by the negative event's being quick, and the third by its being slow.

But, as a further objection to Mellor's argument, it may be said that from 'Leo did not water the flower' it does not really entail 'Leo did not water the flower quickly', or 'Leo did not water the flower slowly'. For, when we say 'Leo did not water the flower quickly', usually what we mean is, contra Mellor's interpretation, that Leo *did* water the flower—it's just that he did it slowly, or not quickly enough. So the negation of the proposition is about how Leo did the watering, not whether he did it at all. In other words, it is not the case that, as Mellor suggests, in stating 'Leo did not water the flower quickly' we thereby apply a positive property, namely being quick, to a putative negative event, namely Leo's not watering the flower; rather, what we do is to apply a negative property, namely being non-quick, to a positive event, namely Leo's actual watering. The so-called negative proposition, 'Leo did not water the flower quickly', interpreted this way, stands without causing any problem[80] for the postulation of Leo's not watering the flower as a negative event, because the proposition is not about the negative event at all.

To this objection, it can be replied that what the objector has above inferred from 'Leo did not water the flower quickly', namely that he actually watered it, is due to something Grice [1989] would call an implicature. By saying that Leo did not water the flower quickly, we do not strictly mean, though may conversationally imply, that Leo watered the flower. This implication is of a pragmatic nature, and can be cancelled if needed. To cancel it, we can simply add—after saying 'Leo did not water the flower quickly'—'Actually, he did not water it at all'. Strictly speaking, the fact that Leo did not water the flower at all is compatible with the fact that he did not water it quickly, as well as the fact that he did not water it slowly. Of course, Mellor's point is not only that the first fact is compatible with the latter two, but also it entails them. And obviously he is quite right about this.

---

[80] Admittedly, under the interpretation it will still cause a problem as to whether there is such a thing as a negative property. But that's *another* problem.

I conclude therefore that Mellor's argument has successfully shown that there cannot be negative events, and hence that to regard absences as negative events in order to solve the problem of absence causation is not a viable open option. Note that in defending Mellor's argument against the second objection we began to talk about *facts*. This will now lead us to another possible solution to the problem of absence causation: viz., to regard absences as negative facts.

Some philosophers, among them are Bennett [1988] and Mellor [1995], have long been arguing for a doctrine of fact causation, according to which facts, rather than events, are basic causal relata.[81] Now, whether fact causation as a general framework of causation is superior to that of event causation is a question I will not go into. The question relevant to our discussion, obviously, is

---

[81] Of course, this is not to say that events can never be causal relata. They may be so in a derivative sense. Mellor's contention [1995: 136], for example, is that an event causes another, only insofar as an existential proposition that states the former explains an existential proposition that states the latter. In other words, c causes e, only if E because C, where 'c' and 'e' are events, 'C' and 'E' are the facts that c and e occur respectively, and 'because' is a sentential connective.

whether adopting the framework of fact causation will facilitate solving the problem of absence causation. At first glance, the answer seems to be 'yes'. Indeed, it appears that the notion of fact causation provides an immediate rescue for the problem of absence causation. For although, as has been argued, absences are neither negative objects nor negative events, it seems hard to deny that they can at least be construed as negative facts, facts that are expressed by true propositions containing 'not' or an equivalent. In our example, even though Leo's not watering the flower cannot exist as a negative event, still the negative fact that Leo did not water the flower is a fact. To better see this, consider again Mellor's argument against the existence of Leo's watering the flower as a negative event. Essentially, the argument consists in saying that the existence of the putative negative event will be undermined by its exemplifying contrary properties: both being quick and being slow. Note that an event's exemplifying a property is itself a fact. So it is a fact that Leo's not watering the flower was quick (or, more naturally put, 'that Leo did not water the flower quickly'), and it is a fact that Leo's not watering the flower was slow ('that Leo did not water the flower slowly'). Put this way, we can say that the existence of the putative negative event, viz. Leo's not watering the flower, is according to Mellor's argument undermined by a conjunction of two facts: the fact that Leo's did not water the flower quickly, and the fact that Leo did not water the flower slowly. Now, the point is that the existence of the negative *fact* that Leo did not water the flower cannot be undermined in the same way, for no fact can be undermined by taking into consideration some other facts or their combinations. All facts, if they are facts at all, are always compatible with each other. So negative facts are immune to Mellor's objection in a way negative events are not. If absences are negative facts, and if facts in general are causally efficacious and negative facts in particular are causally efficacious in particular, the notion of absence causation, insofar as it is understood as consisting in a causal relation in which one (or both) of the relata is a negative fact, will cease to be problematic.

But at this point it is important to note that by 'fact' we can mean two different things. We can mean a true proposition itself, or alternatively we can mean the state of affairs which obtains and which makes the proposition true. In the former sense of a fact, no doubt there are, besides positive facts, also negative ones such as the fact that Leo did not water the flower, the fact that there are no dinosaurs in the University of Reading, the fact that the Earth is not bigger than the Sun, and endlessly many others—if facts are identified with true propositions then of course simply because there are negative true propositions it follows that there are negative facts. But the problem for those who want to construe absences as negative facts so that they can be involved in causal relations is that it won't help much if by 'negative facts' they simply mean negative true propositions. As we have seen, Lewis rejects the idea that propositions can cause and be caused. There is little doubt that he is right about this. Simply because we can *say* that the fact that 'Leo did not water the flower' causes it to be the case that 'the flower died', it does not follow that the causal relation is thus between the two propositions. To make the causal claim substantial, we have to hold the view that there is, *in the world and as an obtaining state of affairs*, a fact that Leo did not water the flower, such that it causes another fact, again in the world and as an obtaining state of affairs, that the flower died.

Borderline Cases (II)

But if we construe a fact in this worldly and truth-maker sense[82], as far as negative facts are concerned a problem arises immediately as to how there can be such a thing as a negative fact in the world. The problem is straightforward. A fact is a state of affairs that obtains. So a putative negative fact, as long as it is a fact at all, must also be a state of affairs that obtains. Yet obviously it is not: a negative fact is negative, precisely in the sense that it is a state of affairs that does *not* obtain. Thus to say that there are in the world negative facts, namely that there are in the world states of affairs that do not obtain, is self-contradictory.[83] In the truth-maker sense of a fact,

---

[82] From now on I will only use 'fact' in this truth-maker sense.

[83] A couple of paragraphs ago I wrote 'the fact that Leo did not water the flower at all is compatible with the fact that he did not water it quickly', and the like. If by this I mean, in the trivial sense of fact, that the negative true proposition 'Leo did not water the flower' is compatible with the negative true proposition 'Leo did not water the flower quickly', what I said is quite correct. But if I mean instead, in the truth-maker sense, that there is a negative fact that Leo did not water the flower, and that there is another negative fact that Leo did not water the flower quickly, and that the two negative facts are compatible, what I said becomes problematic. This being said, in that paragraph by 'fact' I need not mean in the problematic

therefore, we should not really say that there are facts such as that Leo did not water the flower, and, a fortiori, that they are negative facts.

As a realist, I do not find it hard to appreciate the view that there are in the world no negative facts, or states of affairs that fail to obtain. The world as a realist sees it is the totality of everything that exists, or obtains. Whatever fails to exist or obtain is just not in the world, and thus cannot, under the framework of the correspondence theory of truth, make a description of the world—a proposition—true. Since putative negative facts are *ex hypothesi* states of affairs that fail to obtain, there cannot be such things in the world. And it is as simple as that.

---

truth-maker sense nor did I have to mean this in order to endorse Mellor's argument. For the argument's sake, it suffices to say that the negative true *proposition* 'Leo did not water the flower' is compatible, and entails, the negative true *proposition* 'Leo did not water the flower quickly'. What Mellor's argument needs is only an inference between propositions, not an inference between states of affairs that fail to obtain. Mellor is well aware of the two senses of a fact. He uses 'fact' in the trivial sense, and invents another term, 'factum', to mean the truth-maker sense.

No doubt I cannot possibly defend my realist stance here. So I just assume it. And I will be happy enough if it is upon such a strong metaphysical assumption as realism that part of my conclusion rests. That being said, I take it to be another question—and an open question as well—as to whether, from an *epistemic* point of view, the *stipulation* of negative facts is indispensable for us to have a complete knowledge of the world, without which this knowledge would be impossible. Also, it should be mentioned that in denying there are negative facts I have to leave the question open as to what make a negative true proposition true. Presumably all true propositions—or, at least all contingent true propositions—are made true by something in the world. For positive true propositions we can say that they are made true by positive facts. But how about negative true propositions (there are of course a lot of them)? If, as I maintain, there are no negative facts, what make negative true propositions true? To this question there appear to be at least two possible answers. One is to say that the correspondence theory of truth is inadequate, at least for negative true propositions; the other is to say that negative true propositions are somehow made true by positive facts.[84] At any rate, it is neither the only nor an obviously correct option to adopt negative facts into our ontology so as to make negative true propositions true.

In summary, I have in this section discussed several ways of reifying absences: reifying absences as negative objects, negative events, and as negative facts.[85] It turns out, however, that all these options are untenable. I conclude therefore that premise (iii) of the argument from existent causal relata is safe to hold—absences are non-existents.

4.4 Causation and Causal Explanation

In my view the most promising approach developed so far for dealing with the problem of absence causation is the

---

[84] For some recent twists on this issue, see Molnar [2000], Cheyne and Pigden [2006], and Parsons [2006].

[85] Some may take properties as causal relata. But by 'properties' they must mean instantiations of properties, not properties themselves as universals. It seems that absences construed as negative property instantiations are either negative events or negative facts, which I have discussed.

one taken by Helen Beebee [2004][86]. According to our formulation of the problem at the beginning of this chapter, Beebee's approach aims to deny claim (v), viz. the claim that there are cases of absence causation, in which absences are causes and effects. No doubt this claim is a commonsense view backed by intuition. But commonsense can sometimes be wrong, and intuitions can sometimes be inaccurate. If, for good philosophical reasons, it turns out that the notion of absence causation held by many people is some kind of a misconception, under which no genuine causal relation really falls, the canonical thesis that a causal relation always relates *something* will be saved and the problem of absence causation will vanish.

When one tries to reject a commonsense view usually two things need to be done. First, one needs to show *why* the commonsense view is wrong. In this respect, I think enough has been done to show that, since absence causation is *ontologically groundless* (i.e., there is nothing for this kind of causal relation to relate), the view that there is such a kind of causation cannot be right. Second and perhaps more subtly, one needs to show *how*

---

[86] Henceforth all references to Beebee are from this work.

the commonsense view goes wrong. In this respect, Beebee's contribution is to argue that the misconception of absence causation results from a conflation of causation and causal explanation.

The distinction between causation and causal explanation can be traced back to Davidson [1967]. In this classic paper Davidson argues that singular causal statements[87] in the form of 'Dc causes De', where Dc and De are descriptions[88] of two events c and e, need not be, indeed very rarely are, full reports of a causal relation. The descriptions can be partial, but from this it does not follow that the causal relation pinned down by the descriptions is also partial. So for example if in witnessing a car accident someone says that the drunken driving caused the crash, by 'the drunken driving' she is only giving a partial description of the driving. For the driving may also happen to be one-handed, half-minded, etc. Moreover, even if the witness manages to give a full

---

[87] 'Statement' is as Davidson use it. Generally I do not use 'statement'. When I do, by a 'statement' I mean an utterance of a proposition on a given occasion.

[88] Here by a 'description' I mean in a broad sense either a name or a definite description, both of which are used to pick out a particular event.

description of every aspect of the driving, still she can hardly give a full description of what we usually call the 'whole cause' of the crash, which may include, among other things, the rain, the slippery road, and, indeed, the mere presence of another car that the drunken driver ran into. Davidson's point, however, is that what is picked out by the partial description 'the drunken driving', i.e. the *particular* driving, is from an ontological point of view all that is needed to cause the crash. This is because, according to Davidson, the particular drunken driving was *in fact* one-handed, half-minded, in the rain, on the slippery road, and in the presence of another car, etc. The causal work was done by the concrete event, viz. the driving, which had whatever features it actually had. By contrast, our description of the driving—often by way of mentioning those various features—plays no role in causing the crash.[89]

---

[89] Here I only mean to explain Davidson's view, not endorse it. I think that there is a distinction to be made between a partial/whole cause on the one hand, and a partial/whole description of this partial/whole cause on the other. In my view Davidson has difficulty in making sense of this distinction. I will return to this point in next chapter.

The role our descriptions of the driving do play, however, is to figure in causal *explanations* of the crash. When we describe the driving as a drunken one and in the presence of another car we may explain the crash in a way that merely describing the driving as a drunken one will not—say, we may explain why the crash was offensive. And, apparently, when we describe the driving as a drunken one we may explain the crash in a way that merely describing the driving as simply a driving will not. By describing the driving in different ways, we can fulfil different explanatory purposes.

Now, following Davidson's line of thought, Beebee goes on further to suggest that in causal explanation the explanans can be merely *about* the cause event, but not necessarily in the form of a description that picks out the event. That is to say, for the purpose of explanation, anything that can be rightly said about the cause event— or, about the causal history of the effect event at large— can more or less satisfy our explanatory needs. At this point, Beebee is backed by Lewis's thesis [1986: 217] that 'to explain an event is to provide some information about its causal history'. As Beebee [302] points out,

> [Lewis's account of explanation] does not amount to the view that every explanation involves picking out a cause (or some causes) of an event; the way in which causal facts enter into an explanation can be more complex than that. One can give information about an event's causal history...by saying that certain events or kinds of event do *not* figure in its causal history.

It should by now be clear what Beebee intends to say about absences. The idea is that although an absence cannot be a cause, still it, construed as a piece of negative information[90] about an event's causal history, can be of explanatory efficacy. It is this explanatory role played by

---

[90] Here a piece of negative information is just what we usually call a negative fact—i.e., a negative fact in the sense that it is a negative proposition. No doubt negative facts in this sense can involve in explanatory relations, for explanations typically relate just propositions. But since I have mainly used the word 'fact' to mean obtaining states of affairs, to avoid confusion I will here and after only use the phrase 'negative information' when I wish to refer to true negative propositions, not 'negative fact'.

absences in virtue of their being negative information that has misled people into believing that there is absence causation. In talking about absence causation they must have conflated the explanatory role that is indeed played by absences and the causal role that absence can never play.

Interesting as it is, Helen's account is not fully satisfactory. Crucial to Beebee's account is the view that absences construed as negative information *about* an effect event's causal history can explain the event. But what does this 'about' mean exactly?

In our example, suppose that there is a natural causal process leading up to Leo's flower's death— i.e., the causal history of the flower's death. Beebee's view is that among many things *about* this causal history is Leo's not watering the flower. Now, no matter what this 'about' means, it cannot mean that Leo's not watering the flower somehow causally *interacted* with the causal history of the flower's death. For, according to Beebee, absences just do not causally interact with anything. But if Leo's not watering the flower does not causally interact with the causal history of the flower's death, how do we make sense of the fact that his not watering the flower explains the flower's death? By comparison with Beebee's

Borderline Cases (II)

position, note that for those who advocate a *narrow* view of the causal theory of explanation—i.e., the view that, very roughly, causes explain and only causes explain—it is desirable to just regard Leo's not watering the flower as causally interacting with the causal history of the flower's death, such that his not watering the flower causes some event in the causal history, which in turn causes the death. Thus, by way of the transitivity of causation, we can ensure the explanatory link (at least in this context): Leo's not watering the flower explains the flower's death, insofar as Leo's not watering the flower explains a certain event in the causal history of the flower's death, which in turn explains the flower's death. For Beebee, however, to make sense of the fact that Leo's not watering the flower explains the flower's death she cannot adopt this narrow view of the causal theory of explanation, obviously because she cannot allow Leo's not watering the flower to be causally related, either directly to the flower's death, or indirectly (by way of being causally related to some event in the causal history of the flower's death).

It seems that, not being able to resort to a causal relation between Leo's not watering the flower and a certain event in the causal history of the flower's death, Beebee can only say that the 'about'-relation between

Leo's not watering the flower and the casual history is just some kind of a *saying*-about relation. In other words, the idea is that Leo's not watering the flower is just one of the things we can (correctly) say about the causal history of the flower's death. But apparently this 'about'-relation is too weak to make sense of the fact that Leo's not watering the flower, as opposed to some other things we can also correctly say about the causal history of the flower's death, explains the flower's death. Why does not, say, the Queen's not watering Leo's flower, which can also be correctly said about the causal history of the flower's death, also explain the flower's death?[91]

Beebee's view [307] appears to be that things like Queen's not watering the flower does to some degree also explain the flower's death. The problem with this explanation, she contends, is that it is *inadequate*, not that it is wrong. But the problem we are concerned with here is a general one, not limited to the particular case of the Queen's not watering the flower. Obviously, there are a lot of things that can be correctly said about the causal history of the flower's death but nevertheless can hardly

---

[91] For an extensive discussion of this particular issue, see McGrath [2005].

be regarded as explanations of that death *at all*. That the flower is grown on the earth, admired by Leo's neighbour, second to none in the town in terms of its beauty, so on and so forth can all be correctly said about the causal history of the flower's death, but none of them appears to be of any explanatory relevance to the flower's death. Again, perhaps those who advocate the narrow view of the causal theory of explanation can manage to prevent these suggested factors from counting as explanations of the flower's death, by in one way or another ruling them out from counting as causes of the death. But it appears that Beebee's much weaker notion of the 'about'-relation cannot.

Beebee may reply that her primary concern is only with how to make sense of the commonsense endorsement of the causal relation between Leo's not watering the flower and the flower's death—to this question her answer is that people must have mistaken the explanatory role of Leo's not watering flower for its causal role. The question of why Leo's not watering the flower is, but something else about the causal history of the flower's death is not, an explanation of the flower's death, however, is not her primary concern. Indeed, it appears that in discussing absence causation she is generally not obliged to answer any question about the notion of explanatory relevance or adequacy. She can just take the fact that some absences do explain as given, and then move on to elucidate how this given fact matters.

In a sense I agree. I agree that to demystify the notion of absence causation it is just enough to show that an absence's explanatory role should not be confused with its causal role. But I wonder why—here lies my disagreement with Beebee—in order to clarify this confusion we have to appeal to any kind of causal theory of explanation, or for that matter appeal to some kind of 'about'-relation between an absence and a causal history. Presumably, to this question Beebee would answer that commonsense will not, and cannot, confuse just *any* explanatory relation with a causal relation. Unless an explanatory relation is in a certain sense *causal*, commonsense would not confuse it with a causal relation. And unless an explanatory absence is in some way related to an event's *given* causal history, it cannot be properly regarded as a causal explanans of the event. So even though Beebee, unlike the advocate of the narrow view of the causal theory of explanation, does not think that an explanans has to be a cause, still she, following Lewis, holds that the explanans has to be about a cause (or a

Borderline Cases (II)

causal history at large). An assumption behind is that there is a relation/process which we call causal in a primary sense, and then something else about (in some appropriate way) this relation/process can be in a derivative sense called causal too. Thus in the primary sense we have causation, in the derivative sense we have causal explanation.

I disagree. My view, which will be developed in some details in the next chapter, is that a relation's being explanatory is conceptual prior to its being causal, and that causation is conceptually dependent on explanation. As far as absence causation is concerned, my understanding is that commonsense confuses absences' being explanans/explananda with their being causes/effects.[92] Concerning this much I think that Beebee and I can both agree. But in my view it is not part of the mechanism of

---

[92] The reason why this is a confusion is because causation is only conceptually dependent on explanation, not equivalent to explanation. In this sense the confusion is somewhat like some people's mistaking whales for fish: whales are indeed aquatic, but *being fish* is, albeit conceptually dependent on *being aquatic*, not equivalent to *being aquatic*; absences are indeed explanatory, but *being causal* is, albeit conceptually dependent on *being explanatory*, not equivalent to *being explanatory*.

this confusion that an explanatory absence has to be about the causal history of a given effect, unless of course by this 'causal history' we already mean some kind of explanatory history. What makes Leo's not watering the flower look like a cause of the flower's death is only the fact that the former explains the latter. To anchor Leo's not watering the flower to a putative non-explanatory or pre-explanatory 'causal' history of the flower's death will not make his non-watering look more causal. Once, say, someone claims that Leo's not watering the flower is anchored to the causal history of the flower's death so closely and concretely, such that the non-watering occurred all over Leo's back garden and all the time throughout the period of his summer vacation, our intuition will be pushed to disbelieve, not to believe more firmly, that the non-watering caused the flower's death. The explanatory adequacy of Leo's non-watering must be rooted in a certain explanatory context, not in an explanation-independent "causal" history.

Chapter 5

The Explanatory Constraint on Causation

5.1 Introduction: the Explanatory Constraint on Causation and Why It Matters

5.2 Priority: Causation or Explanation?

5.3 The Problem of Selection

5.1 Introduction: the Explanatory Constraint on Causation and Why It Matters

The aim of this chapter is to argue, partly by using materials developed in previous chapters, that a relation's being explanatory is conceptually prior to its being causal. Insofar as this priority of explanation to causation is understood as setting a constraint on the concept of causation, let's call it *the explanatory constraint* (or *Constraint*) on causation.

It is my observation that the *Constraint* thesis, though it echoes something very old[93], has not received nearly enough attention in contemporary discussions of causation. So before setting out a plan for this chapter, let me first say something about how *Constraint*, if true, fits into the bigger picture of the contemporary philosophy of causation.

The fact that causation is intimately *bound up with* explanation is commonly acknowledged. We often explain phenomena by referring to their causes. But *why* it is so is not clear.[94] It appears that anyone who main-

---

[93] In discussing the Four Causes Aristotle [*Physics*: 194b] states his purpose as: 'the point of our investigation is to acquire knowledge, and a prerequisite for knowing anything is understanding *why* it is as it is—in other words, grasping its primary cause.' Note that the term he uses, 'cause', is 'αιτία' in Greek, which means something more close to '*explanatory factor*' in English. It may even seem that Aristotle holds there to be a conceptual equivalence between explanation and causation.

[94] More specifically, there are two related questions involved here. One is why causes explain at all; the other is why causes

tains that we can give an analysis of causation that is independent of the notion of explanation will have to hold it to be a brute fact that causes explain, or hold it by fiat. Neither of the two options is appealing. In my view, the fact that causes explain can be much better understood on the ground that if *Constraint* is true, or, in other words, if a cause' being explanatory is conceptually prior to its being a *cause* at all.

More importantly, *Constraint*, if true, will not only make sense of the explanatory efficacy of causes, but also mean that a major modification to current analyses of causation should be in place. According to *Constraint*, part of what we mean in saying that C causes E is that C explains E. It follows that no analysis of the former that doesn't build upon the latter will be an adequate analysis of causation. This, as far as I know, has not been properly recognized in current analyses of causation.[95]

---

explain effects, in a way that effects do not explain causes. The latter question is about causal/explanatory asymmetry, and will be discussed in some details in Sect. 2.

[95] Horwich [1987: 154-6] briefly considered the plausibility of characterizing a cause as an *explainer* of events, and hence the plausibility of analyzing causation in terms of explanation. He

That we need *Constraint* in analyzing causation becomes particularly obvious when we consider the recent surge of what could be called the disjunctive approach in analyzing causation. Since this is an approach I favour, I shall examine it in some detail[96]. Until very recently, when analyzing causation the general practice has been to figure out a *single* necessary and sufficient condition for causation, be it constant conjunction, counterfactual dependence, or something else. Whenever these analyses faces difficulties—typically, this is when they turn out to be at odds with certain intuitively appealing counterexamples—the general strategy has been to repair it by adding further clauses, rather than to consider the possibility that perhaps what we call

---

didn't carry out such an analysis though. I won't try to do that either. My aim is to argue for *Constraint*, rather than to give a full-blown analysis of causation in terms of explanation. Actually, since (see below) I favour a disjunctive analysis of causation, in my view to analyze causation *merely* in terms of explanation is untenable.

[96] Of course, this is only insofar as *Constraint* is concerned. It is, though interesting, beyond the scope of this book to come up with a disjunctive analysis of causation of my own, or evaluate the current proposed analyses of this kind.

The Explanatory Constraint

'causation' comes in different types which are unsuitable for being analyzed in any single way. The situation, however, has begun to change. It is good to see that more and more philosophers have, for various reasons, come to realize that the concept of causation is more likely to be a disjunctive one, and hence its adequate analysis has to be structured in that way too.[97] I believe that this recent development, though mainly a reaction to all sorts of dissatisfactions with various attempts to analyze causation in a single way (particularly, the Lewisian

---

[97] To give a few examples, Molnar [2000] compares causation as a rational relation with it as an operative relation; Hall [2004a; 2004b] distinguishes causation as production from causation as counterfactual dependence; Sartorio [2005] identifies a difference-making idea as opposed to the idea of counterfactual dependence, both of which capture part of, but neither of which captures the whole, nature of causation; similarly, Kment [2010] identifies causation as determination, by comparison with it as difference-making; Glennan [2010] suggests that causal claims are of two kinds—claims about production and claims about relevance; and, more radically, both McGrath [2005] and Hitchcock and Knobe [2009] come to the conclusion that there is essentially a normative dimension in the concept of causation, which can hardly be captured by a non-normative analysis.

counterfactual analysis), is justifiable in its own right, and is heading in the right direction.

But there is an important consideration that disjunctivists tend to neglect. To appreciate this consideration, note that it is for a plausible reason that many philosophers prefer a single analysis of causation. As is generally assumed in conceptual analysis, in analyzing the concept of causation what we are partly doing is to provide a principle according to which a whole group of superficially different phenomena can be unified. Unification (looking the other way around, i.e. from the principle to the phenomena, this is a kind of generalization) is an inalienable element of any such analysis. If we were simply content with admitting each and every causal relation we come across to be of a different nature, no analysis of the concept of causation would be possible—actually, in that case, identifying any individual relation under review as a 'causal' relation would mean very little, if anything. True, a single analysis of causation, which means to offer just such a unifying principle, may still get the principle wrong, or provide an inadequate version. But a greater danger for the disjunctivist is that he may neglect to provide any such principle at all.

The Explanatory Constraint

Take for example Hall's approach. He declares [2004b: 225] that causation 'comes in at least two basic and fundamentally different varieties', one of which is what he calls 'dependence' (this is in line with the Lewisian counterfactual analysis), and the other is 'production' (this is in line with Fair's energy-flow analysis [1979] and Dowe's more recent analysis [2000] in a similar vein). Putting aside the details of Hall's argument, I suspect that 'fundamentally different' is too strong an expression to use. It might appear that, however much the two proposed varieties may be different, as long as they are both varieties of *causation*, something common must be shared between them. There is no doubt some truth in the claim that there is a kind of causation, i.e. dependence, which is characteristically distinguished from another kind, i.e., production. But if one merely canvasses this distinction, it will leave the impression that it is not clear why the two varieties are both *causal* in the first place, and it may be reasonably wondered whether an appropriate answer to this question is no less important, or probably goes even deeper, than recognising the mere distinction between the two proposed varieties of causation. Hall [2004b: 254-5] is aware of this problem. His reply is that seeking something in common between the two varieties of causation and then making use of this something in common to account for causation in general is a residue of the old univocalist way of thinking. But it seems to me that with regard to this something in common we do not face an all-or-nothing situation. We may have some minimal general condition for any entities to be causally related at all, without elevating the condition into a full-grown single analysis of causation—details can still be worked out, and remain to be seen, in some further analysis in a disjunctive form. Of course, it can be a subtle question as to how minimal the general condition is supposed to be. If I say that two entities are causally related only if they are *related*, this relational condition is obviously so loose that it can hardly be useful for any purpose. On the other hand, if the general condition is too tight then Hall's concern is likely to become real: the general condition may end up becoming yet another single analysis, facing again unaccountable counterexamples.

Can there, then, be a general unifying condition for causation, such that it is not so tight as to disallow enough space for a genuinely disjunctive analysis of causation to be carried out, and yet not too loose so as to supply no non-trivial unification to the sub-analyses of a possible

The Explanatory Constraint

disjunctive analysis? In my view, *Constraint* is a promising candidate for such a unifying condition. It is not too tight, since even if we grant that, according to *Constraint*, causation is a kind of explanation, a lot of things can still be said about how this kind of explanation works in different circumstances, in somewhat different ways; and it is not too loose, since the demarcation between explanatory relations and non-explanatory ones is still substantive. This being said, I admit that the point raised here is very sketchy. The question of to what *exact* extent *Constraint* can serve as the unifying condition for a disjunctive analysis of causation is a question I cannot answer, since an adequate answer has to partly depend on how the disjunctive analysis itself is carried out. My contention is only that, as long as a successful disjunctive analysis of causation has to be combined with a unifying condition which explains why it is certain sub-analyses rather than others that are put together to form the disjunctive analysis as a whole, the idea that *Constraint* may fit the bill as such a unifying condition deserves to be seriously considered.

So much for the theoretical significance of the *Constraint* thesis.[98] Now, obviously the crucial question is whether this thesis is true. With this question in mind, let us briefly review what has been done in previous chapters. In Chs. 1 and 2, I argued that causal asymmetry cannot be adequately accounted for using the frameworks of major theories of causation; in Ch. 3, I argued that causal asymmetry in simultaneous causation and backwards causation can only be made intelligible by taking into consideration explanatory asymmetry; and in Ch. 4, I took on the issue of how to make sense of absence causation, arguing that even in cases where existent causal relata are not to be found, acknowledging the existence of an explanatory relation will still render it prima facie plausible that the relation in question is causal.

All these render support to *Constraint*. But, it is easy to see that while the argument in Chs. 1 and 2 is mainly negative, the argument in Chs. 3 and 4, though positive, only works in some unusual cases of causation. So even if

---

[98] I argued that *Constraint* is theoretically significant to both the univocalist and the disjunctivist. But apparently *Constraint*, if true, can also be adopted even by those who think that no analysis of causation is possible.

The Explanatory Constraint

what was argued in Chs. 3 and 4 is acceptable, whether the explanatory constraint on causation can be generalized remains to be seen.

In the rest of this chapter I will try to show, from some general considerations, that *Constraint* is true. Sect. 2 will deal with a straightforward challenge from the causal theory of explanation, according to which it is rather the case that causation is conceptually prior to explanation. In Sect. 3, the problem of selection, which in my view is fundamental to the concept of causation but cannot be solved without admitting that there is an inalienable explanatory element to this concept, will be addressed.

5.2 Priority: Causation or Explanation?

According to the well-known causal theory of explanation, to explain an event is by definition just to provide, in one way or another, some information about the event's causal history[99]. On this view, without C's causing E it

---

[99] See Lewis [1986: 217].

does not really make sense to say that C explains E.[100] So a causal theorist of explanation will point out that, contra to our proposed explanatory constraint on causation, causation is conceptually prior to explanation; and that instead of saying that explanation sets a constraint on causation, we should rather say that causation sets a constraint on explanation.

Note that the kind of priority the causal theorist has in mind is to be distinguished from an *epistemic* one. It is one thing to say that we always, or even must, get to *know* about a certain causal relation first, and then, by making use of the knowledge we have about the causal

---

[100] The explanation at issue is only a certain kind of explanation, namely the so-called causal explanation, in which explanation is supposed to stem from causation. A causal theorist of explanation does not have to hold the stronger view that causation is conceptually prior to *any* explanation. She can allow that there are non-causal explanations, for example mathematical explanation, but still maintains that, as far as the explanation of empirical existents in general and events in particular is concerned, this kind of explanation is grounded on causation. Since non-causal explanation is not our concern, for brevity when I say 'explanation' I only mean the particular kind of explanation the causal theorist of explanation has in mind.

The Explanatory Constraint

relation, set out to provide an explanation; but it is quite another to say that without such a causal relation in place the corresponding explanation will *make no sense*. The former idea, i.e. the claim that causal relations are epistemic prior to explanatory ones, is obviously too strong. True, often we do proceed in such a way that we get to know a causal relation, and then use our knowledge about this relation to explain (more specifically, use the cause to explain the effect). But it is not unusual to proceed in the opposite direction. In pathology, for example, it is often the case that long before a certain causal connection between a genetic disorder and a disease is established, the genetic disorder has already been invoked to explain the disease. (Indeed, the reason why we set out to discover the causal connection is often because the explanation proves to work well.) This being said, the causal theorist may maintain that the explanation makes sense, only insofar as there is a corresponding relation that is *assumed* to be causal. On this view, even if the causal connection between the genetic disorder and the disease has not been *discovered* yet, this does not prevent us from *assuming* that there must be such a connection. Without this assumption, it cannot be said that the genetic disorder, strictly speaking, explains the disease.

But, causal/explanatory knowledge and the practice of explanation aside, how can the causal theorist justify her claim that causation is conceptual prior to explanation? Since both causation and explanation are highly general and relatively basic concepts, it is hard for her to argue for the priority thesis in any straightforward way.[101] Indirectly, however, there is a well-know argument with regard to causal/explanatory asymmetries that aims to show that causal asymmetry is conceptually prior to explanatory asymmetry. This argument, if plausible, will then render significant support to the view that causation, which incorporates causal asymmetry essentially, is conceptually prior to explanation.

The argument proceeds by appealing to a family of examples. Since all those examples have a similar

---

[101] I don't have a straightforward argument for the priority from explanation to causation either. All my arguments about simultaneous/backwards/absence causation, as well as the arguments I will present in the following two sections, are indirect. As Mellor says [2004: 311], when we can't win by knockout we have to win by points (any relevant points, I understand).

The Explanatory Constraint

structure, for simplicity let us just focus on FLAGPOLE[102]: we can explain the length of the shadow of a flagpole by citing the height of the flagpole; but the reverse does not hold—the length of the shadow does not explain the height of the flagpole. The reason for this explanatory asymmetry, it is suggested, can only be that

---

[102] According to Salmon [1990: 47], the example was invented but not published by Sylvain Bromberger. Note also that FLAGPOLE and similar examples were originally designed by causal theorists of explanation to show that the Deductive-Nomological model of explanation (the D-N model) is inadequate. Roughly, the idea is that while the D-N model in effect construes an explanation as a kind of *inference*, the inference involved in this model can, but an explanation usually cannot, go both ways—that is, according to the D-N model, on the one hand, from the laws and the initial condition the explanandum can be inferred, and on the other hand, from the laws and the explanandum the initial condition (which is part of the explanans) can also be inferred. As a result, the D-N model is criticised for being incapable of making sense of explanatory asymmetry. If so, then the causal theory of explanation will win a point against the D-N model by claiming that explanatory asymmetry is directly derived from causal asymmetry. But, as we will see, things are not that easy for the causal theorist.

the height of the flagpole *causes* the length of the shadow. As Salmon [1989: 47] puts it, 'a flagpole of a certain height causes a shadow of a given length and thereby explains the length of the shadow'. By contrast, 'the shadow does not cause the flagpole and consequently cannot explain its height'. Presumably, the thought is that without the causal asymmetry the explanatory asymmetry does not make sense. If so, causal asymmetry should be understood as conceptually prior to explanatory asymmetry.[103]

As a response to FLAGPOLE, however, it may be pointed out that in order to make sense of the explanatory asymmetry at issue we do not have to appeal to the causal asymmetry. Philip Kitcher [1981; 1989], for example, thinks that he can account for explanatory asymmetry within his unificationist theory of explanation. His unificationist theory is fairly complicated, and for our limited purpose we need not discuss every detail of it. Examning Kitcher's [1981: 525] discussion of explanatory asymmetry, we can summarize his thoughts as follows. A genuine explanation has to fit into our *unified*

---

[103] The thought may also be that explanatory asymmetry is in a certain sense grounded on causal asymmetry. I will return to this point shortly.

The Explanatory Constraint

scheme of explanation. So in considering why the length of the shadow does not explain the height of the flagpole we should not just look at this single case, but widen our vision to consider how explanations of this *type* may be applied in similar cases. Now, supposing the explanandum of the shadow based explanation to be the height of the flagpole, we can see that it is only one of the three dimensions of the flagpole. Sure enough, a similar shadow based explanation can be employed to explain the flagpole's width as well, for the shadow also has a width, from which, other things being equal, we can infer the width of the flagpole. But how are we to explain the flagpole's *depth* by a shadow based explanation? Obviously we cannot. The depth of the flagpole cannot be inferred from any features of its shadow, however much we examine these features in detail. Now, suppose that we adopt the shadow based explanation, in the depth case we shall either have to explain the depth of the flagpole by employing a different type of explanation, or we shall have to give up the explanation. Either way, the shadow based explanation turns out to be restrictive, and cannot be generalized so as to be applicable to a broader range of cases. Moreover, note that the flagpole falls into a general category of opaque objects. We can infer the heights and widths of opaque objects from, among other things, the corresponding dimensions of their shadows. But for transparent objects, which have no shadows, this kind of a procedure is not available. So, not only does a shadow based explanation fall short in explaining the depth of an object, but it can also only be used to explain the height and the width of an opaque object.

By contrast, the usual kind of explanation we employ in explaining an object's height has much more unifying power. As Kitcher [1981: 525] suggests, usually we explain the height of an object by employing a kind of explanatory inquiry that consists in checking the object's 'origin and development derivations'. In general, to carry out this kind of an explanation is 'to describe the circumstances leading to the formation of the object in question and then to show how it has since been modified'. By way of this kind of explanation, not only can we explain the height of an object, but also the object's width and depth; not only the three dimensions of an opaque object, but also those of a transparent object; and, indeed, not only the dimensions of typical material objects, but also the dimensions of some dubious objects such as a shadow (at any rate, the shadow of the flagpole was formed in a certain way and may have been modified in various ways). Considering these factors, we should therefore conclude that the flagpole based explanation, which can be generalized to apply on a wide range of cases, fit into the patterns of our belief system much better than the shadow based explanation, which cannot be generalized to a comparable extent. So, strictly speaking, the problem is not that the shadow based explanation is not explanatory at all; rather, it is that the shadow based explanation is, compared with the flagpole based one, a much more limited kind of explanation. It is this difference between the two explanations' unifying powers that is ultimately responsible for our different attitudes towards them, and that generates the apparent explanatory asymmetry.

But for our current purpose Kitcher's discussion is not fully satisfactory, in the following respect.[104] Granted

---

[104] Kitcher's unificationist theory of explanation is designed to improve the D-N model of explanation, not to compete with the causal theory of explanation. So he does not have to say that his account of the superiority of the flagpole based explanation is incompatible with the causal theorist's account. But here we are interested in Kitcher's unificationist account only insofar as it can be used to provide an alternative base

that his discussion of the limitations of the shadow based explanation is acceptable, his discussion of the superiority of the flagpole based explanation may be vulnerable to a causal theorist's challenge. The point, obviously, is that in Kitcher's account the so-called 'origin and development derivations' of an object still fall into the *causal* history of the object. The causal theorist may maintain that the plausibility of the flagpole based explanation stem precisely from the fact that it cites information about the shadow's causal history—no matter whether it is about the shadow's *formation*, or about its *modification*. So it can be argued that even if the plausibility of the flagpole based explanation is not derived from the *local* causal fact that the height of the flagpole causes the length of its shadow, still it has to be derived from the *broader* causal fact that there is a certain causal mechanism leading to the formation and modification of the height of the flagpole. As Kitcher's account of the plausibility of the flagpole based explanation appeals to the superiority of that *type* of explanation, no wonder the account stands regardless whether or not the height of the flagpole, in

---

(other than the causal asymmetry base suggested by the causal theorist) for explanatory asymmetry.

this particular case, causes the length of its shadow. But the problem is that the superiority of the flagpole-based type of explanation still relies on some broader causal structure of the world.

Perhaps there is a chance that Kitcher's account can be remedied in this respect. Perhaps in his account the reference to 'origin and development derivations' is merely superficial, and the unification superiority of the flagpole-based explanation can be upheld on some ground independent of any causal considerations. At any rate, it appears that the gist of Kitcher's account is that the flagpole-based type of explanation is *structurally* superior, and there seems to be no obvious reason why this superior structure has to be derived from something causal. Suppose, as is not implausible, that some scientific theories can be deemed to explain a certain phenomenon better than other theories, mainly due to the fact that they are better organized, e.g. in terms of simplicity or compatibility with some well-established theories. If so, it is at least not obvious why this better organization has to be derived from consideration of some causal structure of the world.

But to modify Kitcher's account in any significant way so as to fend off the causal theorist's challenge is a project I cannot undertake. Besides, even if some relevant modification of Kitcher's account can be carried out, still the causal theorist may say that her account—i.e. to make sense of explanatory asymmetry by appealing to causal asymmetry—is just another viable option, and is by no means rejected by Kitcher's unificationist account.

There is, however, a more straightforward way to shed doubt on the putative force of FLAGPOLE. It seems to me that the causal theorists are too quick to assume that FLAGPOLE supports their case. Upon reflection, the example may not show what the causal theorist wants it to show, namely that causal asymmetry is conceptually prior to explanatory asymmetry. To see this, first I think we can all agree with the causal theorist that FLAGPOLE, read intuitively, comes down to three points:

> (i) the explanatory asymmetry: the height of the flagpole explains the length of the shadow, but not vice versa;

> (ii) the causal asymmetry: the height of the flagpole causes the length of the shadow, but not vice versa;

> (iii) the asymmetry is explanatory, *because* it is causal.

Now, the crucial point is how to interpret the connective 'because' in (iii). For a start, one may feel inclined to say that the 'because' indicates a kind of *grounding* relation between the explanatory asymmetry and the causal asymmetry, namely that the explanatory asymmetry is in a certain sense grounded on the causal asymmetry. But as far as I can tell it is not easy to figure out what kind of grounding relation exactly is at issue here. As an attempt, I can only think of two relations that might be at issue here. The explanatory asymmetry might be *reducible* to the causal asymmetry, or the explanatory asymmetry might be *supervenient* on the causal asymmetry. Either way, I confess that I have little idea how to make initial sense, let alone argue for, the reductive or the supervenient relations. The burden of argument is on the causal theorist though. So far as I know no causal theorist has defended a reductive or supervenient relation between the explanatory and the causal.

At any rate, the reductive or supervenience relations, if any, are *ontological* ones, and it is not quite clear how they can be related to the conceptual dependence desired by the casual theorist. To simplify the matter, as well as to suit the causal theorist's purpose better, maybe we can interpret the 'because' in (iii), in a more commonsense way, as indicating that the asymmetry's being causal is a *necessary condition* for its being explanatory. According to this interpretation, from the fact that the asymmetry's being causal is a necessary condition for its being explanatory, provided that the reverse does not also hold, it can be safely inferred that causal asymmetry is conceptual prior to explanatory asymmetry. Put generally, the idea is that if an object's being Φ is a necessary condition for its being Ψ, provided that its being Ψ is not also a necessary condition for its being Φ, it follows that Φ is conceptual prior to Ψ. So for example from the fact that an object's being a mammal is a necessary condition for its being a tiger, provided that its being a tiger is not a necessary condition for its being a mammal, we can infer that Mammal is conceptually prior to Tiger.

The Explanatory Constraint

But I find that this reading of the 'because' in (iii), i.e. to read it as saying that the asymmetry's being causal is a necessary condition for its being explanatory is strange. It seems that usually when we say '*A*, because *B*', if there is any necessary conditionality involved at all, what we mean is that *A* is a necessary condition of *B*, rather than, as the causal theorist requires in reading the causal/explanatory asymmetry case, that *B* is a necessary condition of *A*. In order to see this, supposing that I point to an animal, compare the following[105]:

(1) tiger-hood: this animal is a tiger;

(2) mammal-hood: this animal is a mammal;

(3) this animal is a tiger, *because* it is a mammal.

It seems to me obvious that contra (3), it is more natural to say 'this animal is a mammal, because it is a

---

[105] In the following argument I am indebted to David Oderberg for clarification.

tiger'. It is true that an animal's being a mammal is a necessary condition for its being a tiger, and equally true that Mammal is conceptually prior to Tiger. But, for that very reason, we would be more inclined to say that an animal is a mammal because it is a tiger, rather than that an animal is a tiger because it is a mammal. Similarly, in saying that the explanatory asymmetry (the height of the flagpole explaining the length of the shadow but not vice versa) holds, because the causal asymmetry (the height of the flagpole causing the length of the shadow but not vice versa) does, what we mean, if we have necessary conditionality in mind, is that the explanatory asymmetry is a necessary condition of the causal asymmetry.

To put it slight differently, I think that what FLAGPOLE intuitively shows is this. We are inclined to think that the height of the flagpole explains the length of the shadow but not vice versa, and that the height of the flagpole causes the length of the shadow but not vice versa. Further, we are inclined to think that the explanatory asymmetry holds *because* of the causal asymmetry. By this 'because', by and large we mean that the explanatory asymmetry is *derivable* from the causal asymmetry. Now, the point is that this

The Explanatory Constraint

derivability is compatible with the fact that explanatory asymmetry is *conceptually prior* to causal asymmetry. Consider again the Mammal/Tiger case. An animal's being a mammal can be said to be derivable from its being a tiger, despite the fact that Mammal is no doubt a more basic concept than Tiger. By applying the less basic concept, Tiger, to the animal and saying that the animal is a tiger, we convey much more information than merely applying the basic concept of Mammal to the animal and saying that it is a mammal. Since an object's falling under a concept can be derived from its falling under a less basic concept, we can therefore say that the animal's being a mammal is derivable from its being a tiger, and for that reason say that it is a mammal because it is a tiger.

In the same way, a relation's being explanatorily asymmetric can be said to be derivable from its being causally asymmetric, despite the fact that explanatory asymmetry is more basic a concept than causal asymmetry. By applying the less basic concept, causal asymmetry, to the relation and saying that the relation is causally asymmetric, we convey much more information[106] than merely applying the basic concept of explanatory asymmetry to the relation and saying that it is explanatorily asymmetric. Since an object's falling under a concept can be derived from its falling under a less basic concept, we can therefore say that the relation's being explanatorily asymmetric is derivable from its being causally asymmetric, and for that matter say that it is explanatorily asymmetric because it is causally asymmetric, while still holding that explanatory asymmetry is more basic than causal asymmetry.

So the causal theorist's paradigmatic example, FLAGPOLE, is not successful in showing that causal asymmetry is conceptually prior to causal asymmetry. As far as the ontology is concerned, there might be some kind of grounding relation between the causal and the explanatory, but the causal theorist hasn't made this grounding relation intelligible, let alone demonstrated anything conceptually significant based upon a consideration of the grounding relation. If, on the other hand, FLAGPOLE is taken to show that

---

[106] If what we have discussed about the disjunctive approach is true, this richer information should feature in some disjunctive sub-analysis of causation.

The Explanatory Constraint

explanatory asymmetry is a necessary condition for causal asymmetry, or in other words that an asymmetry's being explanatory is derivable from its being causal, then nothing in this example has shown that causal asymmetry is conceptually prior to explanatory asymmetry. On the contrary, the example shows, if anything, that explanatory asymmetry is conceptually prior to causal asymmetry. FLAGPOLE is thus not only compatible with but also complementary to *Constraint*, which says that explanation is conceptually prior to causation.

5.3 The Problem of Selection

Among some long-standing puzzles about causation is the problem of selection. Rooney shot, thereby Chelsea conceded a goal. Usually we say that the shooting is *the* cause of the goal. But upon reflection it is not hard to tell that, besides the shooting, the existence of the goal line, among other things, is also required to cause the goal.[107]

---

[107] It appears that if Davidson [1969: 224] is right in maintaining (sticking with the same example) that the

shooting is *identical* with the shooting across the goal line, it will make no initial sense to say that the existence of the goal line is *also* required to cause the goal. But this needs clarification. According to Davidson, the difference between 'the shooting' and 'the shooting across the goal line' consists not in the (often mistakenly assumed) "fact" that they refer to different events, but the fact that they refer to one and the same event, the shooting, *described in different ways* (the latter expression is a more specific way of referring to the shooting than the former). I agree with this. But Davidson appears to think that because 'the shooting', 'the shooting across the goal line', etc. all refer to the shooting, it follows that the shooting is thus the only, or the whole, cause of the goal. With this I disagree. It seems to me that these are two separate questions: whether, on the one hand, 'the shooting', 'the shooting across the goal line' and etc. refer to one and the same event, the shooting; and, on the other, whether the shooting, no matter how it is referred to, is the whole cause of the goal. An affirmative answer to the first question does not entail an affirmative answer to the second. In my view, the expression, 'the shooting across the goal line', though it *mentions* the goal line, only *refers to*, or *picks out*, the shooting, but not the goal line. And the existence of the goal line, though is not picked out by 'the shooting across the goal line' (let alone by 'the shooting'), is still part of the whole cause (of the goal), which is distinct from the shooting as another part of the whole cause. So while Davidson appears to think that 'the shooting' and 'the shooting across the goal line' are *partial* descriptions of the *whole* cause of the goal, I think that they are *partial* descriptions of (one and the same) *part* of the whole cause of the goal. Davidson's position becomes perplexing when he concedes [1967: 699] that, in contrast to the shooting case, in some other cases an event is 'literally (spatio-temporally)' only part of the (whole) cause. His example of these other cases is Brutus' stabbing of Caesar, which is supposed to be only part of the whole cause of Caesar's death (since Caesar received more wounds than Brutus inflicted). But it seems that the shooting case and the stabbing case are perfectly parallel: Rooney's shooting is a shooting that was actually across the goal line; and Brutus' stabbing is a stabbing of Caesar who had actually received a certain number of wounds. So I don't see how Davidson can in any principled way distinguish the shooting as the partially described whole cause (of the goal) on the one hand, and the stabbing as part of the whole cause (of Caesar's death) on the other. (Note that the spatiotemporal criteria cannot really solve the problem: the existence of the goal line is spatiotemporally separate from the shooting, in essentially the same way as Brutus' stabbing is spatiotemporally separate from other stabbings Caesar received.) For more discussion on this issue, see Vision [1979].

To differentiate it from the shooting, we may want to say that the existence of the goal line is merely a *background condition* of the goal. But on what ground it is justifiable to select the shooting as the cause, distinguishing it from background conditions such as the existence of the goal line?

About this question Mill [*System of Logic*, Book III, Ch. 5, Sect. 3] comments:

> Nothing can better show the absence of any scientific ground for the distinction between the cause of a phenomenon and its conditions, than the capricious manner in which we select from among the conditions that which we choose to denominate the cause. However numerous the conditions may be, there is hardly any of them which may not, according to the purpose of our immediate discourse, obtain that nominal pre-eminence.

And Lewis [1986: 162] seems to agree:

> We sometimes single out one among all the causes of some event and call it 'the' cause,

> as if there were no others. ... I am concerned with the prior question of what it is to be one of the causes (unselectively speaking). My analysis is meant to capture a broad and non-discriminatory concept of causation.

The key thought here is that the kind of distinction we made between the shooting as the cause and the existence of the goal line as a background condition is only of pragmatic significance, and should not be read into the *metaphysics* of causation. In a certain context and for a certain purpose, it is acceptable to pick out a causal factor we are particularly interested in, call it the cause, and distinguish it from all the other causal factors assumed in the background. But as a caveat to this practice, it should be borne in mind that the distinction is pertinent not to the reality of causation, but only to our causal talk. As far as the reality of causation is concerned, the contextually tainted talk of 'the cause', as opposed to that of 'a background condition', does not really make much sense. On this view, the factors we pick out as 'the cause' and 'background conditions' are equal members of the set of a given effect, and each should be regarded, non-discriminatory manner, as *a* cause.

But it seems the non-selective view of 'a cause' thus understood will open a door for too many dubious 'causes' that we would usually feel reluctant to admit. In order to see this, notice that in the example of the goal it is *among other things* that the existence of the goal line is said to be a background condition of the goal. What are these other things? If the suggestion is that they are things like Čech's wrong move in trying to save the ball or the very existence of the ball, then perhaps we can again agree without much difficulty that they are equal causes of the goal, just like the shooting and the existence of the goal line. But how about if things like the presence of air (through which the ball flew), the gravity of the earth, so on and so forth [108], so on and so forth, are also included as causes of the goal? Such inclusions appear to be legiti-

---

[108] For simplicity, in suggesting these putative cause events/states I did not mention the time of their occurrence/obtainment. It goes without saying that the events/states at issue are meant to be individualized partly by the time of their occurrence/obtainment, namely the time roughly when the goal occurred.

The Explanatory Constraint

mate, since those suggested factors are all required in giving rise to the goal and, according to the non-selective view of 'a cause', should be regarded as equal causes of the goal.

But the consequences of adopting the non-selective view go even further. Suppose we admit that Čech's wrong move to save the ball is a cause of the goal. It is easy to see that the goalkeeper's wrong move in turn has its own causes; and these causes must be, qua their being required in giving rise to the wrong move, required in giving rise to the goal, and therefore according to the non-selective view should also be admitted as causes of the goal.[109] By the same token, causes of the existence of the

---

[109] To see how absurd this chain of reasoning can become, note that presumably one cause of the goalkeeper's wrong move is his being in a certain mood prior to the wrong move, and that causes of his being in that mood should in turn also be counted as among causes of the wrong move, and thus among causes of the goal. Now, one cause of his being in that mood can be traced back to, say, his celebration of a goal by his teammate Anelka, which itself was caused, among other things, Anelka's goal. So according to the non-selective view of 'a cause', by this chain of the reasoning it seems that we have to conclude Anelka's goal for Chelsea is among causes of Chelsea's conceding Rooney's goal. And if as a matter of fact Chelsea

ball and the gravity of the earth will also obtain their status as causes of the goal. So the situation we are faced with is not just that synchronically, at the time of the goal or some time immediately before, there appear to be many dubious causes of the goal, but also, diachronically, along all the causal paths[110] that lead to the goal there appear to be too many and even more dubious causes of the goal. To put it another way, since the goal is at the convergence of its many immediate causes, and these immediate causes in turn are at the convergences of their immediate causes, and so on and so forth, it seems that along this line of thinking we will have to conclude that the goal has innumerable, direct as well as indirect, causes, probably at every corner of the universe and certainly all the way back to the beginning of the universe.

---

ended up losing the game, Anelka's goal is thus one of the causes of their defeat!

[110] The term 'causal path', by contrast to the more familiar 'causal chain', is borrowed from Swanson [2010: 225]. When we speak of a causal chain it gives the impression that there is only one; speaking of a causal path does not have this unwanted implication.

The Explanatory Constraint

It may be said that what the above discussion shows is just that according to the non-selective view of 'a cause' an event has a lot more causes than we usually realize. But what is wrong with this? Isn't it rather a virtue of the non-selective view to remind us this *truth* about causation? I disagree, and my complaints about the non-selective view of 'a cause' come down to two points. Firstly, it is counterintuitive. Commonsense treats the striker's shooting, the goalkeeper's wrong move, the gravity of the earth, and etc. more or less differently with respect to whether, or to what extent, they are causes of the goal. The non-selective view of 'a cause', however, treats them all on a par. Of course, some philosophers who claim that what they do is a kind of revisionary metaphysics may be happy to say that their metaphysics of causation has much to teach us and that we *ought to*, resist commonsense and follow their new way of looking at the world. I am not one of them, even though admittedly this methodological dispute may never be settled.

But secondly and more importantly, it seems to me that the non-selective view of 'a cause' taken to an extreme will imply that everything, or at least almost everything, in the past light cone of a given event is a cause of that event[111]. But this will undermine the whole point of the notion of causation. For a given event e, if everything is a cause of e, it appears to be pointless to call anything a cause of e; if *almost* everything is a cause of e, still something's being in this sense a cause appears to be trivial, as opposed to the kind of significance we usually associate with something's being a cause.[112]

---

[111] Here we neglect backwards causation. If backwards causation is true then the idea is that everything in the future light cone of the event is also among its causes. I say 'almost', since the issue at hand also depends on how events are individuated, the question of which I cannot get into.

[112] In an exploration of Russell [1913], Field [2003] raises a similar point, but for reasons I cannot endorse. Judging from what he explicitly says [2003: 440], the reason Field thinks that an event's causes have to include everything that is within the past light cone of the event is basically because he thinks that the non-occurrences of possible interventions of the event must be included among the causes of the event. Using the earlier example, the idea is that, say, Terry's *not* blocking Rooney's shot is a cause of the goal. Now, since Terry's not blocking Rooney's shot is identical with a gravity-of-the-earth-*and*-Terry's-not-blocking event, which is in turn identical with the gravity of the earth, by transitivity of identity we should

The Explanatory Constraint

In short, the lesson we should learn from the problem of selection is this: the notion of *a cause* as we usually understand it has a built-in connotation of selection, which is not merely applicable to the notion of *the cause*, as distinguished from *a background condition*. The problem of selection is puzzling in a way that one misses if one merely concentrates upon the distinction between *the* cause of an effect and a background condition of that effect, ignoring what is involved in something's being *a* cause of the effect. By saying that something can be regarded as *the cause*

---

therefore conclude that the gravity of the earth is a cause of the goal. Now, by extension of this reasoning it is easy to see that we can just combine any arbitrary event in the past light cone of the goal with Terry's not blocking Rooney's shot, or with any other negative causes of the goal, form a conjunctive event in the form of 'the arbitrary event x such that x and Terry's not blocking Rooney's shot', and conclude that any such arbitrary event is a cause of the goal. However, as we discussed in the previous chapter, things like my Terry's *not* blocking Rooney's shot are dubious entities, and should be rejected on the ground that they are ontologically untenable. So in my view it is better to avoid including these negative entities as causes of the goal, not just because they are not causes, but because they are not *anything* (in the world).

insofar as it is contextually salient, one only pushes the problem of selection one step back, but does not really solve it. Originally, we are puzzled by the fact that a certain causal factor is called 'the cause', whereas others are just 'background conditions'. Now, we are told that the distinction is merely contextual, and that both the 'the cause' (so-called) and the 'background conditions' are, from the non-selective view of 'a cause', equal causes. But obviously they are not equal; intuition clearly tells us that some of them are causes, to a degree more than others, and some are not. So with regard to the so-called 'equal causes' sanctioned by the non-selective view the problem of selection rears its head again. We are again faced with a selection between things that appear to be causes and things that appear to be less than causes, or even not causes at all. The non-selective view explains the intuitive distinction made between *the cause* and *a background condition* by saying that the distinction is merely contextual, but an immediate next question is how to explain the intuitive distinction also made between things that appear to be causes and things that

The Explanatory Constraint

don't.[113] At any rate, to deny that there is such a distinction is not an option, since, as we have seen, the denial will undermine the whole point of the notion of causation.

To answer this question, a natural move, as I see it, is to extend the pragmatic understanding of the distinction between *the cause* and *a background condition* to be also applicable to the distinction between things that are causes (of a given effect) and things that are not. In other words, at the level of *a cause*, causation is already contextually sensitive. In view of this, it is easy to see how the thesis of *Constraint* comes into play. According to *Constraint*, part what we mean by saying that something is a cause is that it is an 'explainer'. Now, since we all know that

---

[113] The question I have in mind is not, for a given event e, how we know what its causes are, or, for that matter, how we differentiate all the things that are its causes from all the things that are not. Philosophers need not be concerned with how we know the causes of e, but merely with what we *mean* when we say that some factors are causes of e but others are not. The non-selective view of 'a cause' is too permissive; it amounts to the view that by saying something is a cause of e we mean very little indeed.

the notion of an explainer is a context-sensitive notion, it follows from *Constraint* that a cause qua its being an explainer must be sensitive to context. Otherwise, it is hard to see why, even on the level of identifying *a* cause, our intuition has already been invoked to do some selection work.

But a metaphysician convinced of the non-selective view of 'a cause' may resist this line of reading. Notoriously, he may maintain, in accord with the non-selective view, that one's birth is a cause of one's death[114]. It is interesting to notice, however, how the metaphysician would have to make a case for this strange claim. Lewis for one made a delicate effort, which can be simplified and summarized as follows. You are born, and after some time you die. Apollo does not want you to die, so sends one of his underlings to prevent your death. Suppose that the underling wants to make sure you will not die, and thinks that the best way to prevent your death is to prevent your birth altogether. But he somehow fails to prevent your birth. And as a result you are born, and then die. Now, Lewis contends [2004: 101]: 'When the hapless

---

[114] See, for example, Mackie [1974], Lewis [1986, 2000] and Bennett [1988].

The Explanatory Constraint

underling is had up on charges of negligence, surely it would be entirely appropriate for Apollo to complain that your birth caused your death. And if it's appropriate to say, presumably it must be true'.

My impression, however, is that Apollo's claim (i.e., 'your birth caused your death') appears to be true, because it is said in an appropriate way (i.e., said in the context of the imaginary story)! Lewis has to offer a *context*—a very contrived but vivid context, indeed—in persuading us to believe that one's birth is a cause of one's death. Now, the point is that, out of this explanatory context or similar ones, there appears to be *no* reason for us to believe that one's birth causes one's death.[115] What this shows is precisely that the notion of causation is in a fundamental way dependent on the notion of explanation, and that the thesis of *Constraint* is plausible.

---

[115] Obviously, to answer this question, citing our theoretical needs is misleading. No doubt some theories of causation, Lewis' counterfactual theory for example, will be better off if we believe that one's is a cause of one's death. But a theory—a philosophical one at least—should suit to our beliefs as its data, but not the other way around.

Bibliography

Aristotle. *Physics*

Beebee, H. 2004. 'Causing and Nothingness', in Collins *et al.* (2004): 291-308.

Bennett, J. 1988. *Events and Their Names*, Indianapolis: Hackett.

Ben-Yani, H. 2007. 'The Impossibility of Backwards Causation', *The Philosophical Quarterly* 57: 535-55.

Bigelow, J. 1996. 'Presentism and Properties', *Philosophical Perspectives* 10: 35-52.

Black, M. 1956. 'Why Cannot an Effect Precede Its Cause', *Analysis* 16: 49-58.

Brown, E. 1979. 'The Direction of Causation', *Mind* 88: 334-50.

Cheyne, C and C. Pigden. 2006. 'Negative Truths from Positive Facts', *Australasian Journal of Philosophy* 84: 249-65.

Chisholm, R. 1970. 'Events and Propositions', *Noûs* 4: 15-24.

Collins, J., N. Hall and L. A. Paul (ed.). 2004. *Causation and Counterfactuals*, London: MIT Press.

Davidson, D. 1967. 'Causal Relations', *The Journal of Philosophy* 64: 691-703.

Davidson, D. 1969. 'Individuation of Events', in *Essays in Honor of Carl G. Hempel*, ed. Nicholas Rescher, 216-34, Dordrecht: D. Reidel.

Davidson, D. 1980. *Essays on Actions and Events* (2nd. ed.), Oxford: Clarendon Press.

Dowe, P. 2000. *Physical Causation*, Cambridge: Cambridge University Press.

Dummett, M. 1954. 'Can an Effect Precede Its Cause?' *Proceedings of Aristotelian Society* 28: 27-44.

Dummett, M. 1964. 'Bring About the Past', *Philosophical Review* 73: 338-59.

Ehring, D. 1982. 'Causal Asymmetry', *Journal of Philosophy* 79: 761-74.

Fair, D. 1979. 'Causation and the Flow of Energy', *Erkenntnis* 14: 219-50.

Flew, A. 1954. 'Can an Effect Precede Its Cause?' *Proceedings of Aristotelian Society* 28: 45-62.

Flew, A. 1956. 'Effects before Their Causes?' *Analysis* 16: 104-10.

Flew. A. 1957. 'Causal Disorder Again', *Analysis* 17: 81-6.

Field, H. 2003. 'Causation in a Physical World', in *The Oxford Handbook of Metaphysics*, ed. Michael J. Loux and Dean W. Zimmerman, 435-60, Oxford: Oxford University Press.

Gasking, D. 1955. 'Causation and Recipes', *Mind* 64: 479-487.

Glennan, S. 2009. 'Mechanisms, Causes, and the Layered Model of the World', *Philosophy and Phenomenological Research* 81: 362-81.

Grice, H. P. 1989. *Studies of the Ways of Words*, New York: Harvard University Press.

Hall. N. 2004a. 'The Intrinsic Character of Causation', in *Oxford Studies of Metaphysics*, vol. 1, ed. Dean W. Zimmerman, 255-300, Oxford: Clarendon Press.

Hall. N. 2004b. 'Two Concepts of Causation', in Collins *et al.* (2004): 225-76.

Hausman, D. 1984. 'Causal Priority', *Noûs* 18: 261-79.

Hitchcock, C. and J. Knobe. 2009. 'Cause and Norm', *Journal of Philosophy* 106: 587-612.

Horwich, P. 1987. *Asymmetries in Time: Problems In the Philosophy of Science*, Cambridge: MIT Press.

Huemer, M. and Kovitz, B. 2003. 'Causation as Simultaneous and Continuous', *The Philosophical Quarterly* 53: 556-65.

Hume, D. 1739. *A Treatise of Human Nature*.

Kant, I. 1871. *Critique of Pure Reason*.

Kim, J. 1973a. 'Causation, Nomic subsumption, and the Concept of Event', *Journal of Philosophy* 70: 217-36.

Kim, J. 1973b. 'Causes and Counterfactuals', *Journal of Philosophy* 70: 570-2.

Kitcher, P. 1981. 'Explanatory Unification', *Philosophy of Science* 48: 507-31.

Kitcher, P. 1989. 'Explanatory Unification and the Causal Structure of the World', in *Scientific Explanation*, ed. P. Kitcher and W. Salmon, 410-505, Minneapolis: University of Minnesota Press.

Kline, D. 1980. 'Are There Cases of Simultaneous Causation?', *Proceedings of the Biennial Meeting of the Philosophy of Science Association* 1: 292-301.

Kment, B. 2010. 'Causation: Determination and Difference-Making', *Noûs* 44: 80-111.

Lewis, D. 1973. 'Causation', *Journal of Philosophy* 70: 556-67.

Lewis, D. 1979. 'Counterfactual Dependence and Time's Arrow', *Noûs* 13: 455-76.

Lewis, D. 1986. *Philosophical Papers: Volume II*, New York: Oxford University Press.

Lewis, D. 2000. 'Causation as Influence', *Journal of Philosophy* 79: 182-97.

Lewis, D. 2004a. 'Causation as Influence', in Collins *et al.* (2004): 75-106.

Lewis, D. 2004b. 'Void and Object', in Collins *et al.* (2004): 277-90.

Mackie, J. L. 1965. 'Causes and Conditions', *American Philosophical Quarterly* 2/4: 245-55, 261-4.

Mackie, J. L. 1974. *The Cement of the Universe*, London: Oxford University Press.

McGrath, S. 2005. 'Causation by Omission: A Dilemma', *Philosophical Studies* 123: 125-148.

Mellor, D. H. 1995. *The Facts of Causation*, London: Routledge.

Mellor, D. H. 1998. *Real Time II*, London: Routledge.

Mellor, D. H. 2004. 'For Facts as Causes and Effects', in Collins *et al.* (2004): 309-23.

Menzies, P. 1999. 'Intrinsic versus Extrinsic Conceptions of Causation', in *Causation and Laws of Nature,* ed. Sankey, 313-30, Dordrecht: Kluwer.

Molnar, G. 2000. 'Truthmakers for Negative Truths', *Australasian Journal of Philosophy* 78: 72-86.

Mill, J. S. 1843. *A System of Logic.*

Oddie, G. 1990. 'Backwards Causation and the Permanence of the Past', *Synthesis* 85: 71-93.

Papineau, D. 1985. 'Causal Asymmetry', *British Journal for the Philosophy of Science* 36: 273-89.

Papineau, D. 1992. 'Can We Reduce Causal Direction to Probabilities?', *Proceedings of the Biennial Meeting of the Philosophy of Science Association* 1992: 238-52.

Parsons, J. 2006. 'Negative Truths from Positive Facts?', *Australasian Journal of Philosophy* 84: 591-602.

Pears, D. F. 1957. 'The Priority of Causes', *Analysis* 17: 54-6.

Peterson, P. 1989. 'Complex Events', *Pacific Philosophical Quarterly* 70: 19-41.

Price, H. 1992. 'Agency and Causal Asymmetry', *Mind* 101: 501-520.

Price, H. 1994. 'A Neglected Route to Realism about Quantum Mechanics', *Mind*, 103: 303-36.

Reichenbach, H. 1956. *The Direction of Time*, Berkeley: University of California Press.

Russell, B. 1913. 'On the Notion of Cause', *Proceedings of the Aristotelian Society* 13: 1-26.

Salmon, W. C. 1980. 'Causality: Production and Propagation', in Sosa and Tooley (1993): 154-71.

Salmon, W. C. 1990. ***Four Decades of Scientific Explanation***, Minneapolis: University of Minnesota Press.

Sanford, D. H. 1976. 'The Direction of Causation and the Direction of Conditionship, *Journal of Philosophy* 73: 193-207.

Sartorio, C. 2005. 'Causes as Difference-Makers', *Philosophical Studies* 123: 71-96.

Sosa, E. and M. Tooley (ed.). 1993. *Causation*, Oxford: Oxford University Press.

Swanson, E. 2010. 'Lessons from the Context Sensitivity of Causal Talk', *Journal of Philosophy* 107: 221-42.

Taylor, R. 1973. *Action and Purpose*, New York: Humanities Press.

Tooley, M. 1987. *Causation: A Realist Approach*, Oxford: Clarendon Press.

Tooley, M. 1997. *Time, Tense and Causation*, Oxford: Oxford University Press.

Vision, G. 1979. 'Causal Sufficiency', *Mind* 88: 105-10.

von Wright, G. H. 1971. *Explanation and Understanding*, London: Routledge and Kegan Paul.

Wertheimer, R. 1968. 'Conditions', *The Journal of Philosophy* 65: 355-64.

www.ingramcontent.com/pod-product-compliance
Lightning Source LLC
LaVergne TN
LVHW051827080426
835512LV00018B/2750